T7

C000271572

Green Fields and Pavements

Green Fields and Pavements

A Norfolk Farmer in Wartime

Henry Williamson

Illustrations by Michael Loates

The Henry Williamson Society

Collected writings of Henry Williamson previously published by
The Henry Williamson Society:

Contributions to the Weekly Dispatch, 1920–21
Days of Wonder
From a Country Hilltop
Genius of Friendship: T. E. Lawrence
A Breath of Country Air, Parts I & II
Spring Days in Devon
Pen and Plough
Threnos for T. E. Lawrence

This collection first published 1995

The Henry Williamson Society
14 Nether Grove
Longstanton
Cambs

Text © The Henry Williamson Literary Estate 1995
Illustrations © The Henry Williamson Society 1995
Frontispiece © Oswald Jones 1957

Standard edition ISBN 1 873507 07 0
Limited edition ISBN 1 873507 08 9

Typeset by Cambridge Photosetting Services
Printed and bound in Great Britain

CONTENTS

EDITOR'S NOTE AND ACKNOWLEDGEMENTS

This collection of articles reprinted from the *Eastern Daily Press* was originally compiled by myself in 1971, with an over-ambitious plan for a privately printed, limited circulation edition. Henry Williamson, when approached for permission, vetoed the idea in a friendly letter: '. . . the printing costs of the proposed (somewhat irregular) publishing venture [must be] totally uneconomic . . . So the little venture discussed at Spode House last Whitsun must, I fear, be abandoned.' And in another letter, 'I am sorry but it is not practicable to publish the *Eastern Daily Press* articles. [They] are listed to appear when I collect my newspaper articles, in due course.'

While Henry never did get round to collecting his newspaper articles (a daunting task, in view of his huge output), the Society founded after his death has published several such anthologies over recent years.

Perhaps it is befitting therefore that now, in this centenary year of his birth, The Henry Williamson Society is publishing this book. Editing has been kept to a minimum, although some explanatory footnotes have been added whenever appropriate, while the date each article was published is also given.

I would particularly like to thank Oswald Jones for providing the portrait of Henry, and Mick Loates for his beautiful drawings, which add so much to the book. The Henry Williamson Society gratefully acknowledges the permission of the Trustees of the Henry Williamson Literary Estate and Eastern Counties Newspapers Limited for their permission to reprint these articles.

John Gregory

AN ARTIST'S TRIBUTE

by

Mick Loates

At some time in our lives nearly all of us find some kind of personal affinity, inspiration or solace through the work of a creative spirit. Nearing my half century I must surely be humbly qualified to reflect on those details which have had such a prodigious influence on my own life and work. There were and are great painters, some lost to the centuries, one or two still alive that transferred, into my psyche, a sense of extreme beauty way beyond everyday appreciation. The same can be said of musicians and writers.

Somewhere in the midst of my second decade I chanced upon the work of Henry Williamson and throughout the following ten years I read little else. From the intimately observed beauty, sadness and ultimate tragedy of *Tarka* and *Salar*; the schoolboy humour of *The Beautiful Years* and *Dandelion Days*; the complex romanticism of *The Pathway* and *The Gold Falcon* to *A Chronicle of Ancient Sunlight*. Some titles I read with an obsessiveness six times over, gleaning further wonder and inspiration on subsequent readings.

Over the intervening years I have continued to read Williamson having found no other author who imparted so much personal emotion and inspiration. One identified with the author through so many facets; childhood locations and pursuits, an appreciation of the beautiful and a compassionate drive for truth and humanity.

From the window of my studio today I look out onto a panorama of rooftops and walled gardens sloping steeply to a quay and beyond to green hills flanking the east and west of a south Devon estuary. It's all a far cry from the south London suburbs I knew during childhood and youth. My life has been much enriched through the prose of Henry Williamson.

My small contribution to this delightful ephemeris represents nothing further than a modest visual enhancement of a page, but the drawings are a personal tribute to Henry in this his Centenary Year.

Kingsbridge 1995

FOREWORD

by

Bill Williamson

Upon reading these articles in this centenary year of my father's birth, I realise that I have forgotten neither the events nor the people who worked for us in those far-off days. I suppose I learned a lot of my growing up from them, working as I did on the farm for some six years, starting in September, 1939, at age thirteen-and-a-half.

I spent the first winter with a very dear man, Jimmy Sutton. Jimmy, a man in his mid-fifties, looked after the cattle, the sheep, and the pigs. It was a full time job, especially in the winter, when all the stock were in the yards, and had to be fed and bedded every day of the week.

The mangolds, used for cattle feed, had to be sliced up in a root-cutter, turned by hand, mixed with chopped oat straw, and some sugar-beet pulp, then carried to the feeding troughs in a bushel measure, called a 'skep'. Water was laid on to the central yard only. It was carried in pails to each yard as needed. Hay was stored at one end of the 'premises' in the large haybarn and had to be carried out either in forkfuls, or in a large net. I accepted it as being the way things were done. Not until later, when I worked for a year on a Canadian farm, where the animals were kept on the ground floor of a large barn, with all the hay, straw, and feed stored above, and dropped down through chutes, did I realize how inefficient and time consuming it all was.

In Spring 1940 I was judged ready for the tractor. Under the watchful eye of Jimmy's son Bob, I learned how to handle the Ferguson and two-furrow plough. It was then on to seed bed preparation, sowing, and eventually, harvesting.

Everything that first year was an adventure. Helping with the threshing, hauling the heavy watercart to the old Burrell steam engine, moving the threshed grain to the Corn Barn – all was a new experience.

It was sometime in 1941 that Henry began his reclamation of the many 'marginal' areas of Old Hall Farm. There are about seventy acres of low lying meadowland attached to the farm, with an extensive drainage system of 'grupps', or ditches. These had become choked with weed and silt, and required cleaning. Dick Curzon, 'Powerful Dick' of the farm books, was hired to pull the grupps. He worked hard all one summer, clearing many hundreds of feet, thus lowering the water level on the meadows. He stayed on that winter, working in the hay barn, grinding feed, or helping to winnow seed corn. Many of the farm hedges were overgrown, and for about a fortnight I helped Dick cut and lay an old thorn hedge encircling part of the premises.

Once, when it looked like rain, Dick said, 'Not yet, haven't seen the Greyhounds.' Sure enough, soon low grey clouds were scudding over, and it was raining. He didn't mind hard work, the 'hard graft' as it was called, but he didn't like the stooping, bending work in the root-fields, so when the grupp pulling was finished, he left to work for someone else.

About this time, Bob, the Teamsman/Steward, decided he would go elsewhere, and then Jimmy left as well. This left us with one good man, Norman Jordan, who had been with Henry since 1937, and stayed to the end. Norman's nephew, Douglas, came at this time to look after the stock, and stayed until the end of our tenure.

By now, most of the tractor work was being done by myself. The second tractor would be used when someone qualified was available. This would be brother John during his school holiday periods or sometimes an adept Italian P.O.W. Perhaps Kathie, the Landgirl would help out or even an Army or Airforce type on leave, who had come over on a literary quest and found himself helping with whatever was pressing at the moment.

Nineteen forty-four saw the ploughing of both the Hall Hills and the two far meadows. It was too much. We worked that tough old ground for a month in the spring of '45 with the result that we never got onto the regular arable until it was too late to expect a proper crop. Labour for the beet-lifting was a problem, and Italian 'Co-operators' arriving in gangs of twenty or more, would collectively do about as much in a day as one hard-working village woman.

Small groups were different. For the last harvest, I would pick up a squad of three or four fellows in the Alvis at their campsite on Cley marshes, and return them each evening. Once I was invited to share their supper of spaghetti, with a delicious sauce and bread they had baked themselves.

It was soon after this that Henry decided to sell the farm. I think it was as much a relief for him to leave for his newly found house in Suffolk, as it was for me to leave for a new job, and eventually, Canada.

I saw him not more than half-a-dozen times after that, and both of us were rather restrained and ill-at-ease. Lastly, we met for a few minutes at Twyford Abbey where he spent his final days. Then the telephone call came from John in August 1977, followed by the last goodbye at Georgeham.

Canada, January 1995

The Seed Goes In

For five months the farmer has waited for this moment of shining sun and drying fields. He has waited for the spring, but not as some others in the world have waited. The farmer does harm to no one by his work and scheming. He may appear to be a dull, heavy fellow, with no 'intellectualism', no idea of what poetry is about, or what shape the New World should take when the war is successfully finished. But the life in him is the life of the fields and meadows, of his beasts and seeds and implements. He is natural man on his natural earth. He has his being – his imagination gives him life – in the seeds of his husbandry.

The seed in our Big Barn has been 'dressed' during the rainy days of the past winter. On our farm this dressing took the form of old one-eyed Billy turning the handle of a wooden machine which shifted the seed-corn from one sieve to another, while a wooden propeller-like affair winnowed the heads of thistle and other light bodies left by the threshing machine. The seed is dressed to purify it, to let the little dwarf kernels of shrivelled corn drop away with other impurities. Small corn grows small corn; it is the falsest economy to use poor seed.

As Billy turned the handle of the creaking machine Bob poured bushel measures of barley into the top of the dresser; while my small son shovelled into a bushel measure the good seed which slid out of the end of the machine. (It was made about 1895, that dresser; bought at an auction for 12s. and home-repaired. Before the war small farmers could not afford to buy such luxuries as modern dressers.) The good seed in the bushel measure was lifted by Norman and tipped into an old butter churn. Then amongst the seed a two-ounce measure of mercuric compound was carefully scattered. This was a deadly poison, and must be handled carefully.

A baffle of crossed pieces of wood fitted in the churn threw the seed about when the lid was clamped on and the handle turned. The

1

object is to impregnate the skin of each grain with the powder which will kill the spores of any fungus or other disease lodging on the grain. Perhaps you have seen ears of wheat, in July, turned to smutty brown powder? This is what the farmers call 'stinking rust', 'bunt', 'black-head', or 'blight'. About four million spores may be lodging on one single grain of corn! So Norman turned the old churn slowly, to throw the seed about, and for the fine poison-powder to slither over each grain. Afterwards he must wash his hands before eating his dinner.

The corn was then sacked up and the window left open for the white owl to fly in at night and take the small rats and mice which might gnaw the sacks. Good jute, those sacks, and it's been a struggle to get them looked after properly, after the two decades of neglect in British farming. We have few rats, as they are scientifically kept down by an infection or plague which affects only rodents. Once every six weeks a man arrives with packets of small sandwiches, of bread and paste, which he drops by the holes under the sixteenth-century walls. The rats, cunning beasts, would perhaps avoid bread left so conveni-ently for them; but they feel safe by having to bite through paper. The result is an epidemic; and so the good white owl seldom flies into our barn; but just to be on the safe side the window is left open for him.

(Note: – In the 'New England' after the war, when farming will be prized by the nation equally with its mercantile trade, I suggest that rats, which waste millions of pounds worth of food a year, should be obliterated by a nation-wide campaign, using the modern scientific method of spreading plague amongst them.)

2

Our seed-corn is ready in time. The harrows are reset and repointed, for drawing deep cultivation strokes through the frost-fretted furrows of the autumn ploughings. Yesterday I walked over my fields in the warm sunshine, noting with satisfaction how the stiff clay has been reduced to a nice, friable tilth by Jack Frost. In 1939 the frost came too early, and we were caught out; the fields were not ploughed until February, 1940, when sticky layers of clay were turned up in rows. Many harrowings and many rollings could not produce the fine moleheap-like tilth which barley growers so desire. Only the frost can do that on heavy land; the frost which expands the water-particles in the clay as it freezes them into ice, leaving in the thaw a spongy mass which in the winds of March dries to an almost light soil as the harrows pass.

In two days, I told myself, this land will be fit for the harrows. If we come on it now the feet of the horses and the wheels of the tractor will 'sump' in and press the fretted clay particles into sticky layers again. Meanwhile, we will rush on with the spreading of the mud heaps on the next field – about 400 tons of rich black mud. That should grow some corn!

It is always a question of time; always a rush. That field has to be ploughed, it is light soil, and will present no seed-bed problem; but we have only one tractor, and it can't plough Spong Breck while also harrowing Hilly Piece. We'll have to work from first light to last light, that is all – my small son and I, and take turns on the Ferguson, with its twin-ploughs operated hydraulically: the ploughs of the future.

For the corn must and shall go in to time. All things have their seasons; and corn sown late can seldom catch up to yield a full crop. These splendid autumn ploughings, all done by the 14-year-old boy last October and November, must not be wasted. The men demur at working on Saturday afternoons, and to ask them to work Sundays would cause a little mutiny, so we will do the work ourselves. I ploughed one field on Sunday in 1939, and the wheat failed – due to excessive cold rains followed by severe, prolonged frost, which killed the new-sprouted seedlings – but the bailiff is convinced it was a judgement for Sunday working. Submarines may be sinking wheat-ships, Heinkels flying overhead (for a few moments before going down before the circular saws of the Spitfires), but much of British farming is still of the Old Testament period. Perhaps when the New Britain comes along, and the rats are all gone with the weeds and the swamps, and a fine new informative technical education arises with the new system, then the old obstructive inhibitions will be no more. They are a part of the wretched cottages, a perpetual hangover of the century-old national neglect of British agriculture. I believe in the future, I believe in pedigree corn and beast, I believe in the genius of English people, which shall transcend the dark things of the past in the light of nature, and in the integrity of human truth.

March 12, 1941

Farming in War Time

Hitherto on those occasions when someone from the Continent of Europe has wished to alter its economic and financial structure by dispossessing the bankers of Lombard and Threadneedle streets, British farmers have benefited by the increases in agricultural prices. Superficially, this corrective war appears to be no exception. Quite recently, to give an instance, barley has been bought for as much as 380/- a quarter. The same quality of grain in 1923 fell as low as 38/- the quarter. And two wars ago, after Napoleon had closed the Baltic, but just before he started on what was to have been the final triumph in the march against Russia, wheat rose to 126/6 the quarter of two sackfuls. That was the highest price paid for wheat in 500 years.

I began my little farming career during a depression. In 1938, when I took my first samples of grain, somewhat tremulously, to the Corn Hall at Norwich, one of the first things I saw was an old farmer in disgust spilling his sample of unwanted barley on the floor. Even the sparrows, who must have been almost the best-fed birds in the county, seemed to take no interest, as they perched on the iron framework of the roof. Hearing the old fellow muttering to himself, I drew nearer, to hear how he took it. His actual words were, 'That's a rum 'un.'

Wheat, which in 1941 was 65/6, may go to the Napoleonic peak price in this Hitlerian war, but I doubt if it will make farmers (other than smallholders of up to 100 acres or so who pay little or no tax) feel any the more secure. Indeed, it seems to me, from what I hear, that the bigger farmer you be today, in a sense the worse off you find yourself.

During the harvest of 1941 I met one big farmer, and in reply to a question about the saving of his barley he told me it did not matter to him if his barley was a good malting sample or not. It was a wet harvest; on our field called Fox Covert the Squarehead II wheat, standing during so many showers in the shock, was beginning to chit

5

in the ear. That for me was an anxiety, for I was proud of the good corn I had grown, and was hoping to make a nice price for it as seed. (My overdraft was £1,000.) As for my barley, I recognised that, with the rains and mists and the good seed-bed which had started it well, it looked like being a first-class sample.

The big farmer, however, was depressed by the fact that most of the fruit of his labour would be taken from his farm. 'I'm farming for the country, not for myself,' he said. It did not matter to him if his barley made the best price as a Norfolk Fine Ale sample, or merely the price of coarse, steely stuff, fit only for pig meal.

I do not know how many acres he farmed, but it was several thousand. Now let us suppose that he had altogether 6,000 acres and that he had farmed his land before the war with sheep and bullocks to maintain the fertility of his fields, following the usual rotation, and had managed to make both ends meet, and perhaps a little more: indeed he might, with mutton and beef and wheat a dud market, easily have lost money. When it came, therefore, to war-time taxation, he would not be allowed much profit, for in war-time he would be assessed on the basis of his best year in peace-time. The authorities were amenable in cases of pre-war losses: they put a limit of £1,500 on a farm's profit. Thus our man, farming 6,000 acres, is allowed today to keep £1,500, or 5/- an acre profit. Of this 2/6 comes off as income tax, leaving him with 6,000 half-crowns with which to feed, clothe and educate his family, to provide liquid capital to pay his wages and all other expenses of running his farm for another year, and to buy any new machinery that is needed. For new machinery is not allowed as an expense: payment for it has to be made out of those 6,000 half-crowns. If his land were mortgaged he would not be able to pay off his mortgage. I know one farmer who did this, but his relief at at last being out of debt was short-lived, for he had to mortgage his land again in order to pay his E.P.T.*

During the first two years of the war the theme of Farmer Giles as a good fellow was almost popular. Several 'national' newspapers, no longer concerned with the sensibilities of revenue-providing advertisers who might have had other irons in the fire, declared that farmers were grand fellows in the front line and their tractors were doing as much to win the war as tanks and bombers. The same theme was sung in the last war. Readers of Adrian Bell's classic farming

* Excess Profits Tax

trilogy, *Corduroy*, *Silver Ley*, and *The Cherry Tree* (surely the most readable books in the English language) will remember the post-war depression and bankruptcy among Suffolk farmers following on the popular war-time sentiments of 'Never again must English farming be allowed to decay,' etc., etc. This slogan reappeared in 1940, and was sung during 1941, but just now the theme is modulated somewhat. In some places the farmers are looked upon as a greedy lot, making large profits, and the trend of popular (that is 'national') newspaper argument is inclining to the 19th century idiom of 'To get money for our factory goods we must buy in the country where we sell, and that means cheap imported food; for we'll see to it that by loans and credits abroad we remain top-dog and so control the currency in our favour.' When the war is won the argument of these financial gentry will be, 'Food from English farms is dearer than imported food: Mr Townsman, why pay more than you need? Didn't the farmers simply coin money during the war?' So Farmer Giles will feel the cold draught and Hodge will shog off to the factory in the nearest town for a job.

I had the honour of dining the other night with a gallant commander of troops who, before the war, was on the Stock Exchange. After our victory, he said, all the blether about the home markets first would disappear like yesterday's snows in today's sunshine, and the grand days of 'free for all' would return. Wasn't he just looking forward to it! Booms and slumps, and the clever ones getting away with it: that was the life! He was quite right: it was the life. The operative word, as Beachcomber would say, being 'was'. Many other things too, one might venture to say, will have their existence only by the past tense. Individualism, so often an euphemism for noncooperation, may disappear with small fields and small farms, narrow roads and crumbling cottages, impure water supplies and impure mental supplies, and all the other contributing causes of the things that were – and were not good enough. For an incurable optimism within me insists that British leadership is potentially the finest in the world, and that when the British people have overcome that which for so long has divided them, they will give a lead to the world which will compensate for (and incidentally explain) the blunders and derelictions of the past.

March 30, 1942

War and Peace

Below me I see a bit of England that for many years has been let go. It is a cottage garden. There are many overgrown shrubs and bushes about the area, and the place is without form or design; or rather, it is that unpleasant thing, a pightle or parcel of land neither truly wild nor truly under human order. In a word, it has been neglected.

Between the cottage gardens a hedge of ash and elder straggles tall and ragged. Elder is the poor man's hedge; a few sticks pushed into the ground, and soon there is growth. This growth is a substitute for a hedge. Elder grows rapidly, with sappy hollow stems that are useless for pleaching or as a barrier for stock. It does not form a hedge; it cannot be tamed and ordered, like beech, thorn, or holly. Elder is a tree-weed. The man who makes a 'hedge' of this weed is the man who stops the gaps of his 'hedge' with worn-out bedsteads, rusty bicycles and disused earth-pails. That was the standard of hedge-making in the village when the war broke out.

For, generally speaking, the village was losing heart, and had been verging on a rural slum for some years before September, 1939. We all know the reasons now – or haven't we realised them fully yet? It is difficult to see ourselves as the historian will see us, as some genius, perhaps unborn, may re-create these times as did Tolstoy in his mighty novel, *War and Peace*. That Russian nobleman shut himself away for over five years and with infinite care and patience and the power to endure, set himself to bring alive, within the pages of his story, the peasants and the landowners, the ministers and the priests, the battles and the sufferings, the loves and deaths and joys and tragedies of an entire Russian generation; more, of an entire European age. There was Napoleon, with his new order for Europe, directing battles and regarding the dead and the wounded – all in *War and Peace*. Napoleon, who failed in Africa, frustrated by the British Navy, who, turning East into Asia, found the grave of his Army – and his hopes – in the snows and ice of Russia.

No wonder the book is out of print, with many hundreds of thousands of readers in England wanting to read it. 'Didn't you fight with bows and arrows in the last war?' asked a youth joining the A.T.C.,* with a laugh, to the old soldier of 1914–18. How then did they fight in A.D. 1807? Napoleon used the same technique, of massing his cannon at one point and making a lightening break-through, pouring in his heavy yet mobile troops, and turning the flanks of his opponents, a veritable pincer-movement. He was successful in battle after battle, beating the Allies who didn't under-stand this new way of fighting. His men rode over bridges, a general or two at first, smiling and dismounting, and talking with the enemy, declaring that the war was over, a truce had been made, and peace would shortly be signed. The astonished Allied sentries then see a French regiment marching over the bridge; not a shot is fired. They don't understand it. They watch the French gunners spiking their guns. Thus Napoleon crossed the Danube, the war still on, and not a shot fired to stop him. Pure bluff.

Was that how Hitler crossed the Maas in May 1940, and so turned the Maginot Line? It was all done before, by the Ogre of Europe, who was said to eat human flesh for breakfast, who won battle after battle and defeated nation after nation until in the end his armies were spread out over all the conquered Continent, and far into Russia . . . and that was the beginning of his end. He went too far. When he lost Africa, he lost the war; he cracked his teeth in Russia, where at last they learned to counter his encircling tactics, his lightening assaults, what an Austrian general of those times called his *blitzen* tactics.

Napoleon tried to break the hold of the English bankers on Europe. He was blockaded. He retorted by a counter-blockade. He tried to starve out England. He closed the Baltic, and no more Russian wheat went to Britain. The price in Britain promptly rose to 80s. a coomb. Napoleon offered a prize for a sugar substitute, and from Poland came a weed from which was bred a plant called a beet-sugar. He offered a prize of 10,000 francs to any chemist in Europe who found a process of making bicarbonate of soda out of common salt. Somebody won it. He started silk mills at Lyons and Lille to make a substitute for cotton, which could only come to Europe from America by way of British ships. And in 1815, when Napoleon was finally taken, he made a prophecy. He said: 'These British will rue the day that they

*Air Training Corps

did not co-operate with my system. In a hundred years they will be at
war with a great European power, arising from the valley of the
Rhine.' A British officer, one of his guard in St. Helena, that lonely
ocean isle, was deeply moved at the ex-corporal's death, feeling that
something great had gone from his life, that he would never find
again. All most interesting for us today.

Who will write the *War and Peace* for this age? Will he show the
decaying art of husbandry in England between the two Germanic
wars, and relate it to cheap food imports, foreign loans, rusty British
ships laid up in toll-free estuaries for many years suddenly being sold
as scrap to Japan, German coats being made from wood, price-cutting
in British industry, dole queues, the burning of wheat in America and
the dumping of herrings in Scotland while children in British slums
starve; the conscientious objectors of 1914–18 becoming fire-eaters
of 1939–43, ex-Service men of 1914–18 with decorations for bravery
becoming pacifists of 1939–43, the 'decadent democracies' becoming
totalitarian in their efficiency and the totalitarian States decaying into
inactive democracies? Will he show the Baltic being closed, and
barley going to 180s. a coomb in 1941 when it was 16s. in 1938? All
the effects of peace related to all the causes of war? The boy on the
tractor longing to fly a Spitfire, and the fighter-pilot with several
'gongs' longing to farm quietly somewhere, and never see a gun
again? Hitler believing passionately in one thing and doing its
opposite? And why? And how the bull-thorn supplanted the elder and
the bedstead in the little hedges of England?

I hope to live to read it.

April 19, 1943

Faith, Hope, and Clarity

As a journalist of some little experience all kinds of books and pamphlets come my way, and I am struck just now by the great number of societies and groups, with their manifestos and plans, now arising in Britain, and for one declared purpose – for the making of a new world *after* the war. Most of these are private endeavours, as opposed to official schemes or intentions, or rather suggestions. There is a plan to abolish all rents, and by this simple act apparently to free the land and the people of 'an age-long tyranny.' The sponsor of this plan declares that she visualises 'a kind of gold-rush on a certain day, rents being taken off at, say, noon on Saturday, and millions from the towns racing forth to take up their heritage of earth.' It will, the claim runs, solve overnight the problems of slum and urban congestion, etc., and result in a general improvement of the national health, etc. In a few broken bones and black eyes, too, I fancy.

Well, that's one of hundreds of schemes, ranging from the above fantasy to the abolition of banks, from the nationalisation of land to its division among labourers in small parcels of thirty or forty acres each. Other ideas are that Britain cannot possibly carry a population of more than twenty million people, and there should be compulsory emigration to the colonies... a Customs (or economic) union between the United States and the British Commonwealth, thus bringing back North America to the Mother Country, after a century or so of secession. The prodigal returns, with dollars.

Scores of similar schemes have come by post during the past months, as they have gone to thousands of other addresses; and while it would not be wholly true to say that they cancel one another out, they do reveal a lack of unity. This disunity arises from an unknowingness (ignorance is too crude a word) of the view-points of others. Thus the lady who believes that rents should be abolished, and in ardent imagination sees from the ensuing scramble for land a

11

new harmony arising, does not seem to know it would start a thousand little civil wars. It is easy to laugh at these ideas as being cranky, but all pioneers had a crank; Florence Nightingale, the Wright Brothers, Marconi, Jenner, Pasteur, and innumerable other inventors and discoverers, all were cranks in that mass mediocrity was opposed to them. What we can allow from all these schemes is that there is a general dissatisfaction with things as they are; the old order of things was not good enough, and we want a new civilisation.

In the village where I live, I sometimes hear talk of this new world *after* the war. I heard similar talk during the last war. It is significant that I have never yet heard of this world-to-be coming about through great work on the part of *everybody*. 'They' ought to build new cottages. 'They' are responsible for wars. 'They' profit from wars, and therefore 'they' keep wars going. 'They' want the labouring man kept down; 'they' won't work properly. ('You can't say anything to them nowadays; they'd leave if you did,' – *audite* any farmer.) It is always 'they'.

Which came first, the chicken or the egg? Which comes first, the men who are said to be working not so hard as they might, or the farmers who are said to want to keep the labourers down? What was the cause of the ruinous state of farming before the war, the bad farmers or the economic system which gave the farmers bad markets? Who was responsible (who was 'they'?) for the bad markets? Where does the truth lie?

I am no better than my neighbour; I, too, have blamed 'they'. I have my own ideas for a new world. Yet something is lacking in all these schemes. It is something that was lacking in our national life before the war – Unity. We were divided, class against class, business against business, section against section, town against country. There were many aspects of truth, local truths which were untruths a few miles further on. The labourers had their truth; the farmers had theirs; so did the landowners; and the urban financial gentry.

Norfolk farmers wanted a fair price for their barley; Midland farmers wanted cheap barley for their pigs. East Anglian farmers wanted a fair price for beef, in order to tread their straw to make their muck to grow their corn and sugarbeet; the towns wanted cheap meat, which came by way of refrigeration-ships from South America. Whose truth, the cold storage interests or the East Anglian beef interests? The fields went down to 'grass', the men were stood off. Were the farmers to blame, by thus averting bankruptcy? Some farmers kept their men on, and were ruined; and their land degenerated. Which was better, to conserve the land, or to give the labourers work on an uneconomic basis?

I believe that men can only live truly by being fair; and first, men must learn to see fair. In the old world, the old order, the old way of thinking, fairness to one section was often unfairness to another section. I think that hope for a better order can come only through all of us knowing the other person's point of view. Both sides in a controversy can be right; many conflicting view-points can be true at the same time; and this I believe to be the message which, seemingly at the time, came to such a tragic ending over nineteen centuries ago. Faith, Hope and – *Clarity*.

April 26, 1943

News of England

A wounded General exchanged recently with other wounded soldiers, British and Italian, spoke of the deep hunger of our men abroad, not only in the prison camps, but all over the world, for news of England.

I know well this longing for one's own place, for one's own people, this *nostalgia* or home-sickness for the reality of one's true self. When a soldier in the African desert calls to another, 'What about a pint of mild and bitter now, mate?' he is not merely reacting from his present thirst, but desiring all that which in the past – the remote and dreamlike past – meant freedom to him. His mind may not make any clear picture, or even a swift-broken succession of pictures; he will see nothing definite, for nothing of the spirit is definite. And unless he is introspective he will hardly be aware of the authenticity of his spirit. Even to himself he will not be able to declare any definition of the dreamlike past. It is the function of the artist, or the poet, to do it for him.

Just as it is hard to imagine friends who are dead, so the past can never be recalled, even by the extraordinary concentrative power called genius, as a continuous whole. Broken flashes of feeling which almost verge on the visual never quite succeed in becoming even fragments of pictures. Insight is but the essence of the past, of each man or woman's past, playing on the present.

We see a child weeping because its toy is broken; we know what it feels only because we have in the past suffered the same thing. And the man or woman who has what is called deep understanding of humanity possesses that insight or understanding only because he or she had meditated on, and realised, his or her own past acts and circumstances. 'The fool sees not the same tree that the wise man sees,' wrote Blake; and Shakespeare, in the character of Hamlet, utters a variation of the same truth, 'Only he who has not felt a wound laughs at a scar.'

When the General spoke of the deep hunger of our men abroad for news of England he defined this news as details of ordinary life, the so-called little details which will light up the spirit of the exile's former freedom or ordinary existence. 'What about a pint now, mate?' cries the tank-driver, emerging from the intense metallic heat of his machine, and in that instant his spirit is home again, in a moment as timeless as the pulse of the radio beam. He neither smells nor sees nor hears in his mind; the instant flash which brings a clutch to the heart is not to be analysed. Our soldier does not see the bar-room or the dart-board, nor the friends talking contentedly as they sit on the settle; he does not hear the talk of hoeing, the discussion about the piece-rates for beet that are being paid that season, he does not recall babbing for eels in the mill pond, or see the duck which have flighted to the black mud channels in the snow-covered marshes. It is such details as these, of his old familiar life, that the ex-countryman, now soldier or sailor or airman, longs to connect with, to contact in his subconscious mind or spirit, in his soul . . . which lives its own life, apart from present circumstances, in its own freedom, in its own *home*.

There was a gale at the beginning of April and mile after mile of roadside hedges were yellow with straw. Tufts of it hung on telegraph lines, looking like straw birds perching on the wires. It clogged the brambles, it strewed the arable; most of the stacks in Norfolk were reduced to half their bulk and shape. What the boy in Africa who once worked on the smallholding wants to know is where father put the stack last harvest, and if he is short of litter, and where was Mum when she saw it, and what the Sunday afternoon walk was like, and whom she saw. Details of no importance in the old life before the old life was ended; one pint was like another, one evening of May like another evening; but not now that the horizon of life is beyond the leagues of sea and sand and sky, these details are of life itself, the very food of the soul. The baby crawling on the floor when you went away now rides a tricycle, and has sown his first seeds (radishes) in the garden, and the first radish that came up the little tot wanted to send to you in the desert. With sharp poignancy such a detail in a letter brings home faces, fields, streets, all with a powerful emotion that is (though few know it) the very essence of poetry, of art, of all that is permanent, of all that is indeed immortal in the true life of England overseas. It is the little things of life that make truth.

May 3, 1943

A Cuckoo Singing

A bird flew in level flight across the clover field and alighted on a red bough near the top of one of the pines standing at the edge of the wood. I was standing by the new-laid hedge, and as it passed me on its flight I heard a throaty noise, as though it were squabbling with itself, coming from the slightly curved beak. It was a bluish-grey on the back, and its breast was a dull white barred with lines of black. '*Gabble-gobble-wobble*,' and I was reminded of an old country-woman, in a poke bonnet, scolding a boy who had been shooting at her bee-skep with a catapult . . . myself being that boy, in a village not far from Cromer.

The image of the old woman came to me before I could think, or fix the thought in my head; and with it the memory of the legend that in olden days the cuckoo was supposed to be let out of an old woman's bag in mid-April; whence it began its cry which is known to everyone.

I watched the bird on the reddish-brown bough of the pine tree, as it sent call after call across the layer to the barley fields beyond. The cuckoos of this hill have a reputation for fierceness that I found hard to believe until a man working for me, who is usually truthful in such things, declared that as a small boy he and another were going that way to school, one May morning, when they heard the cuckoo's voice coming from the wood; and, imitating the cry, the boys were startled to see the hawk-like shape gliding down towards them, where they stood in the sunken lane which led up the hill. It was making a gabbling cry, as of anger, and seemed to be flying straight for the face of one boy, who had been mocking its call. 'I dursen't go that way any more,' said my informant. 'The bird seemed to strike at us again and again, and we ran away, frightened. We never heard any other cuckoo singing up there, either. It seemed all alone.'

Now birds and animals vary, as do men; some seem more gentle than others, less alert, some milder, others fiercer, some quick, others slow. Why did this bird show anger of its mocker? All the cuckoos I have seen have been inoffensive, hardly less apparent than their voices; yet here was one behaving like a female brown owl on watch during the day by its young in a hollow tree. It was a male bird, and it was a frustrated bird, and when at last (I imagine) it heard another male calling, it behaved in a way a bull behaves when it has been shut up too long away from its natural companions.

Down in the farm is a patch of comparatively new flint and brick work, replacing that which gave way before one bull which deemed it had stood in the yard, alone, too long. (The effects of sexual frustration are general knowledge today; and a very prominent European figure of our times will make most interesting biographical material when the present-time obfuscation of fact gives way to the clairvoyance of history.)

The cuckoo in the pine tree went on calling, and I wondered if any female in the neighbourhood was watching from some similar vantage point, spying out the nests, or the nest sites, of her future dupes or stooges. The cuckoo, as has been proved by Mr Edgar Chance in his capital book, *The Secret of the Cuckoo**, watches and waits and inspects the nests of its foster-hens-to-be, and at the right moment glides down, squats on the nest, lays an egg, takes one of the nest-builder's own eggs in its beak, and flies away with it.

I have seen a cuckoo do this, flying away from a pied wagtail's nest in a summer-house with a grey egg, which it swallowed as it sat on the branch of an oak tree a few yards away. Looking in the wagtail's nest, I found the larger cuckoo's egg, which had not been there a minute before, when I had happened to peer in.

Mr Edgar Chance has watched and photographed the female cuckoo, many female cuckoos, searching for nests. The female waits until the right moment before gliding down in that intent, hawk-like glide, to lay her egg and then away. By watching one female, Mr Chance discovered all the nests which she had selected as the cradles of her imminent offspring. Cuckoos have territory, like the owl and the rat, the squirrel and the badger, the trout and the crayfish, the tree and the plant, the bootlegger and the vice-racketeer of the 'roaring 'twenties' of prohibitionism across the Atlantic. In fact, every living

---

*Edgar Chance wrote both *The Cuckoo's Secret* (Sidgwick & Jackson, 1922) and *The Truth about the Cuckoo* (Country Life, 1940). It is not clear which book is referred to here.

thing, or organism, or human organisation, from great industrial nation to the little man with his rag and bone (pre-war) round in the cities, needs territory, or living space. They struggle for food and they struggle for immortality (sometimes called love), and if one or another individual or racial instinct be frustrated we see a cuckoo going crazy or, on a larger scale, we hear the bursting of bombs.

May 10, 1943

The Little Ports

Once the coast here was lower, and the sea came up the channels with every tide, bearing wooden ships burthened with cargoes which were unloaded on the quays and taken inland in wagons. Many sailed away with grain, to other ports in England, who wanted the North Norfolk barleys for beer. Gold was the medium by which payments were made, but not the paramount purpose of the exchange. The general principle was that of exchange of goods in the community. Northumbria wanted barley to make beer to feed the coal-miners, and East Anglia wanted coal. So barques with coal left Newcastle and drew into Cley and Blakeney and Overy and Burnham, and returned with barley and wheat. The farmer sent his loaded wagon, painted with bright colours, drawn by four horses, from his black barn door to the quayside granary of his merchant, trusting him to pay the right price for the grain, and often as not the wagon came back with a load of coal or other goods.

Water was the only means of moving heavy goods over long distances, for the roads were full of holes, and many of them not properly repaired since the Romans left centuries before. The coastal traffic of England, with the lesser movement on canals, was the chief means of trading; thus we were from the earliest times a maritime race, a little continent on our own, made up of all the adventurous elements in Europe... hardy Danes, pioneering Vikings, sturdy Icelanders, clever Phoenicians, thorough Romans, tenacious Normans. Small wonder then that as the scope of sailing ships increased this amalgam of virile European stocks – grafted on the easy-going native Celts – known as the English, sailed to other coasts and landed there and fought or made friends with the natives and eventually, with the coming of steam, consolidated the greatest Empire in the world; and as a nation, remained undefeated and uninvaded through scores of wars during nearly a thousand years.

Whether these little familiar ports had silted up in the flow of tides or had remained open, their trade would have declined eventually; for with the technical advance of the machine, and of industrialism with it, the old trade on a basis of exchange and mutual trust, the old honest life of craftsmanship pre-eminent as a standard of life, was superceded by competitive big business, and the idea of seeking monetary profit anywhere in the world. Counterfeit quantity succeeded quality; the old standards decayed; speculation and cunning took the place of stability and hard productive work. These changes were gradual and came about through so many intervolved circumstances that only the clearest and strongest minds were able to see how the new idiom of profit for the sake of profit was likely to despoil the native English character. Financial interests ruled the world, and those interests came largely into cosmopolitan hands.

Usury became paramount over craftsmanship; the materialists triumphed over the artists. Much of the literature of the nineteenth century was disguised social criticism; and only towards the end of the century did this criticism of materialism begin to perceive that the economic system was at the base of the artists' dissatisfaction. Later, books like John Galsworthy's *Man of Property*, though often sentimental at base, and satirising the men and manners of dividends instead of the God Dividend, began to make it plain to the ordinary man that the chasm between spiritual hopes and materialistic reality was too great.

Whether the little ports of the Norfolk coast had silted or not, it is probable that they would have fallen into disuse, due to causes hitherto beyond control. I write 'hitherto', because today we are beginning to control, through necessity, some of those causes. And the will to alter the conditions of the causes is beginning to form itself in the minds of millions. For myself, I rejoice to see economy and orderliness, where before was waste and disorder; I am happy by the sight of hedges being trimmed once more and arable being cultivated, of slum children growing sturdy and natural in the countryside, of the feeling of resurgence underlying the circumstances of war, of the chastening knowledge that we were all responsible for something that was not good enough, and therefore are now aware of our attitude towards the future.

These thoughts came into my head as I cycled along the coast the other day, surveying the effects of the greatest gale of the war.

May 17, 1943

Topsy-turvydom

How queerly war reverses nearly everything of our peace-time lives and thoughts! It has often occurred to me that nearly everything today is turned upside down or inside out. A letter this morning from a publisher set my mind off on this train of thought. Here is a sentence from his letter:

> Absurd as it may sound, my chief fear sometimes is that some book or other that we publish may turn into a best-seller! What a desperate remark for a publisher to have to make!

A publisher, generally speaking, leases the copyright of a book he decides to publish, from the author, and pays him a royalty on all copies sold, usually about a shilling on a book which is sold to the public at 7s. 6d. The publisher pays all costs of setting-up in type, printing, paper, binding, advertising, and sales distribution to the shops. Publishers back their fancies and invest their capital in the books they decide to publish. If an edition of a book costs, say, £300, and the publisher sells only 300 copies, he will obviously lose most of his money expended on its production. He may publish a book, knowing it is good, and yet realising that it will probably lose money, at least for the time being, but that in years to come the author will be famous and then he will recoup himself by reprinting it. He may launch twenty or more books in a spring or autumn season, always hoping that one of them may be a winner, when it will pay for those which do not sell enough to clear their costs of production. And it is every publisher's dream (or was) to have a best-seller.

When this happens he will concentrate on advertising it in many different ways. A 7s 6d. novel probably pays for itself when it has sold 1,200 copies; after that figure the profits begin to increase in proportion to the number sold. Every copy read with enthusiasm sells one or more copies; readers begin to advertise it by saying to their friends, 'You must read so-and-so, it's a grand book,' and so the snowball is rolled down the slope, gathering momentum and weight as it goes. Perhaps plates are made from the original type – impressions, as wax takes the imprint of a seal – and several printers may be turning out sets at the same time. The more it sells the more it is 'pushed'. Will it sell 100,000 or more copies, like *If Winter Comes*, *All Quiet on the Western Front*, and *Good Companions*?

But not today. The publisher dreads a best-seller. He knows his paper ration won't stand it. The printers won't be able to cope with it. It is the same in other trades. Wine merchants buy up bins of wine at the few rare sales, and then resell to their old customers at pre-war prices. They know that war-time money or profits are not real wealth or profit; the E.P.T. sees to that. So they sell at a 'loss', which means that they buy with cash which otherwise would go in taxes. They want to keep their old customers, for the war will not last for ever.

Coupons are nearer real wealth than paper money in a State which is fully controlled by the Government. You see advertisements in the newspapers asking customers NOT to try and buy the advertiser's goods. Everything topsy-turvy; buildings are hurried up, and then swiftly destroyed; ships are built only to be sunk. A nation which had a large section of its population near the starvation-line in peace-time, when the problem was too much food in the world and too many 'consumption goods', is now being fed better than ever before in its history – and at a time when only the scantiest stocks of food are available in that country! Moonlight, which was a symbol of romance and human tranquillity, now is a portent of fear and human misery . . . the bomber's moon.

Width of sympathy and understanding in peace-time have no place in war-time. Judicial virtue, when expressed, can be dangerous. A man will not be popular who understands how the hounds hunt and also how the hare feels when it is running away. Above all, he must not attempt to explain to the hare what is the view-point of the hound, or of the whipper-in, or of the huntsman, or of the field-master; nor must he utter to any of the hunters the truth of the hare's authentic feelings, or reactions to being hunted. He will be called two-faced, or even three-faced, or four-faced. An artist, to interpret life truly, must see all things as they see themselves, as it were; as the sun, with its infinite sympathy to all forms of life, sees those forms of life. Artists have to shut-down in war-time, at least in their fuller comprehension or divination of people and of events. The true artist has always lived dangerously; witness the lives of the martyrs, of the discoverers, of the scientists ... Galileo, Pasteur, Abraham Lincoln, Florence Nightingale, a hundred others.

War-time is one great paradox. 'Water, water everywhere, and not a drop to drink.' (No prize for guessing where that applies at the moment.) Shopkeepers conceal their goods, hide them away from the windows, in case people want to buy them. And who in peace-time would think of milking a motor car? I can assure you it has been done, and often, during the past twelve months.

May 24, 1943

Along the Coast Road

I cycled along the coast road, free with a delightful sense of solitude, and so came to an area which probably was painted in peace-time more often than any other East Anglian district. Wide marshes and reedy dykes, villages of pantiled roofs and crumbling flint walls – many broken by traffic – corn barns with their tall, black double-doors, cattle yards, an old windmill, fields green with barley, distant sea and low, ragged line of sandhills under an azure sky of a clarity unsurpassed in any other English coastal landscape.

In peace-time this narrow coastal road, winding up and down hills and through quiet little villages, was worn smooth and dark with oil droppings and the continuous whirr and rolling of the rubber wheels of motor cars. This early summer day I had the road to myself and peaceful it was; the sun was shining in silence, a broad and shimmering silence that took me, in an instant, back to the wondrous summers of my boyhood.

I sat down on the grassy verge of the road, beside a cluster of poppies, and tried to project myself into that age before the last war when the summer days seemed a broad and endless glide of golden lights despite the classroom and the hours spent away from the light of the sky. What was missing today was the glare of the sun in the pale and dusty road. Ah, that was the difference, the heat of the dusty roads, their quietness, the sleepiness of the broad summer day of light and shade and slow drifting cloud!

The cuckoos and the larks were singing, and a grey horse was moving over the brow of the hill, drawing a wheeled hoe down the lines of roots. The axle wanted grease, and squeaked a little. Then I heard the clip-clop of a trotting pony and down the road came a dog-cart, with flashing red wheels and black body and two polished candle-lamps with fronts shaped like silver horse-shoes. Yes, it might have been a scene of 30 or more years ago, except (to the observant eye) that the barley was not so sturdy a plant, and the ewe flocks were

25

infrequent, when they had been common sights. Then it seemed that the power of the sunlit silence, broken only by birdsong and the receding clatter of the pony's hooves, was being withdrawn from the earth, to be bound by an invisible power and turned into a swift and massive movement. Squadron after squadron of four-engined bombers flew, heavily in their laden strength, towards the north-east. After them came the fighters in line of sections, so fast to see that the azure air seemed to be a liquid streaming from the blade-tips of their wings.

No, it was not the same country any more, it was not the countryside of the olden days. 'This blessed plot, this realm,' the 'precious stone set in the silver sea,' was still there, but temporarily it was overlaid by 'this aircraft carrier lying off the coast of Europe.' Two telling phrases indeed; the one written by one who loved England, the other by one who hated her. Hatred passes, but love endures; the lark over the barley will be singing in the sunshine when the swift shadows are forgotten.

To the road again, and over a slow river where reeds rustled in the breeze, and up the steep hill to another village, where stood a grey church tower and a smaller tower, like a child beside its parents. Not much good going down to the quay; the sailing boats were stored away until happier days, and the terns on the Point would be flying undisturbed, except for the gulls marauding along of their own wild world. Men no longer watched birds on the gem-like shores of England; they watched for other wings from the fortified aircraft carrier.

At length I came to a green valley, with a view of meadows and woods and a field of corn, and a small river moving sluggishly below the road. Now water always interests me, for I am a fisherman who prefers peering for fish and water-flies and plants almost more than setting about the catching of fish. I have taken salmon in Scotland (or killed fish, as they say), and with both fly and spinner have landed brown and sea trout in the rivers of Wales and of Southern and Western England. In Canada, with French-Canadian guide, I have gone on *portage* through the woods, carrying a canoe and flung the great and gaudy flies called Parmachenie Belle, Orange Fish Hawk and Fan Wing Pink Lady after the red-bellied brook trout that roll up out of the deep and dark lakes.

While I was sitting there I met the owner of the river, who was also a fisherman*. He had a tale of woe to tell about that little stream.

*Williamson himself. The weekly pieces appearing between April 19 and June 14, 1943 were written by him under the pseudonym of 'Jacob Tonson', hence the use of this device.

Although it was chalk country, this brook was not a pure chalk-stream, in that it did not flow direct out of the springs from the chalk, like the famous Test and Itchen. Pure chalk streams are not affected directly by rain storms, so their water is always crystal clear. This little Norfolk stream, declared my acquaintance, was now a canal being used as a drain. Years ago, it had a firm bottom of gravel or chalk; today it was overlaid by a foot and more of mud. The mud came from the road culverts, and from over sixty other drains (in about six miles of its length) which poured in various forms of pollution. Even Council house drains did this, despite the Rivers Pollution Act and the Public Health Acts, declared my informant, speaking with some bitterness. In addition, the river had been artificially widened by constant pulling of mud and the trimming of banks, until the rate of flow was diminished and all scouring or self-cleaning of the bed by the action of water was diminished, and a maximum of silt was deposited. The greater the widening, the greater the accumulation of mud; and so the muddy river-bed was in places nearly 18 inches higher than before the North Norfolk Rivers Catchment Board began its operations about a dozen years previously. Meadows which before had been good grass, now were studded with rush clumps, rank and inedible water-grass flourished, and the clover, so good for making good firm beef, had almost died out. As for the trout, which once had been numerous and gay and lively, these were infrequent. Many were black, the colour of eels.

'To me, this pollution is symbolic,' he declared. 'It is part of the general neglect of so much in this precious realm. One day the brook will run clear again, even as salmon will leap once more in the Thames by London Bridge.'

May 31, 1943

The Falcon's Flight

I have been reading lately the autobiography of a young actor who fought in the action of *Prince of Wales* and *Hood* against *Bismarck* and *Prinz Eugen*.* Some readers may recall Emlyn Williams' sensitive and telling broadcast after the nine o'clock news a year or so ago about his friend Esmond Knight, how at Denham studios one day Knight was looking at birds in the sky during an interval of the making of a film about Drake; and how, after the film was made, Esmond Knight said he wanted to join the Navy; and how he saw the *Hood* go up in a stupendous sheet of light, and then all was darkness and he was lying in hospital in Iceland, where the nights were long with the midnight sun; but his own travail was longer, for he was blind.

Esmond Knight has now written, or dictated his life story, which is published by Hutchinson†. It tells of his boyhood in Kent, his schooldays at Westminster School, his early struggles to succeed as an actor, first at the Old Vic, and then in the West End, his marriage, his experiences in UFA films at Neubabelsberg studios in the pinewoods outside Berlin, his training and flying of falcons with his

---

*This action took place in the early hours of May 24, 1941, in Denmark Strait, midway between Iceland and Greenland. The *Hood*, a battle cruiser completed in 1920, was hit by a salvo probably fired by the *Bismarck*, and blew up with a huge explosion between the after funnel and the mainmast. She sank within three or four minutes, and there were only three survivors. The *Bismarck* was not to last much longer: after being crippled by Swordfish flying from the *Ark Royal*, she was sunk by the British fleet on the morning of May 27, 1941.

†*Seeking the Bubble* (1943). Esmond Knight (1906–1987) partially regained his sight – 'rather like looking through clouds', he said – and was acting again within two years. Although his sight progressively deteriorated he contrived to appear in a great variety of plays, helped both by his unwavering enthusiasm and his strong memory; he would spend hours learning every corner and distance of the sets on the stage, so that he could move as freely as if he had no handicap. His many films included *Henry V*, *Richard III*, *The Red Shoes*, and – *Sink the Bismarck*.

uncle, Captain C.R.W. Knight, the well-known lecturer and photo-
grapher and owner of 'Mr Ramshaw', the eagle, on Salisbury Plain;
then the war and the thrilling, aweful, heart-bumping moments
preceding the action in which *Hood* blew up, and very soon afterwards
his consciousness flashed out.

It is a brave little book, written with a light touch, and it interested
me particularly because once I met the author, although he probably
will not remember the evening, about ten years ago, when we talked
behind the scenes of Percy Robinson's play, *To What Red Hell*, in
which he was then acting. I was looking for an actor to play the part of
a war-torn poet, and I remember both Esmond Knight and Robert
Peiseley, two young actors, telling me that Stephen Haggard was the
very man for the character. I never met Haggard, although many
times was on the point of so doing; and now this sensitive actor and
poet is dead, of pneumonia in North Africa. It seems almost like a
personal loss, for I feel I knew him, despite the fact that we had never
met. Stephen Haggard wrote a book about a young girl that I thought
very good, called *Nya*, one of those books that one can read again and
again, and always with fresh interest. It is probably out of print, but
I hope the publishers (Faber & Faber) will reprint as soon as possible.
It is worthy of their Faber Library.

I was talking the other day with another acquaintance of Esmond
Knight, who is mentioned in his autobiography. There was an argument over a meal of crayfish and hock they once had in a Berlin
restaurant, about the speed of the peregrine falcon's flight. Knight
declared that he had timed the level flight of a peregrine, on Salisbury
Plain, by the aid of the speedometer of his car, which could not
exceed fifty miles an hour; and he had kept up with the falcon (a tame
one). The other man had written a book in which he had stated that
the speed in level flight of the wild falcon sometimes exceeded a
hundred miles an hour. There is a difference, of course, between the
power and flight of a semi-tame bird, taken as a fledgeling or eyas
from its nesting rock on some steep cliff, and kept in a stable or mews,
and that of a wild and mature bird. Indeed, it might be that there is
only the slightest basis for comparison. On that occasion, according to
Esmond Knight, the conversation ended by the other man declaring
dogmatically that speedometers were 'notoriously inaccurate,' after
which nothing more was said; but I would like to have been present at
the talk, for the speed of these birds has often intrigued me.

It is, of course, hard to decide at what speeds birds as a species will

fly, for they vary as do men and animals; but I have seen a peregrine falcon, hanging a thousand feet above the Needles, fall suddenly with startling speed, and in a moment appear to be on the point of dashing into the sea; then zooming up as though shot from a great catapult and with a sharp sweep round and with no perceptible flicker of wings, 'wait on' at its pitch a thousand feet above the waves again. In a few seconds it has 'stooped' at a pipit or some small bird struggling against an off-shore wind, missed the tiny object, and hurled itself up once more as though it had power to reverse the force of gravity. I have watched the bird turn and glide, apparently level, at an incredible pace, dip down and fall like a piece of dark slate, turn in a steep curve and, without pause or wing-beat, shoot away in level flight for a quarter of a mile in a few seconds, and all that without the least apparent effort. It might have been made of lead, for the sheer directness of its shift.

As for the grand stoop of a strong falcon, this is something to be seen, but hardly to be believed! Once, in Cornwall, I watched one slipping down the sky at a slight falling angle, and through glasses I saw it increase its glide or stoop until in less than half a minute (it seemed) it had gone out of sight over the mainland, which was three miles distant. There were woods beyond, where wild pigeons lived, and I could visualise it falling on one, I could feel the shock of the strike knocking off the pigeon's head. This is no exaggeration; twice have I seen a partridge, flying downwind at speed, hit by the swifter dark barb, its head spinning off in a scatter of feathers, the body hitting the ground with a thud, and, as it bounced slightly, to be caught in a dark flick of impact and be borne away.

Compared with the slow and hesitant flight of a falcon, recently hooded and immewed, and thrown off from a gauntleted wrist at a slinking rook on Salisbury Plain, this description of a wild bird's flight must seem exaggerated; but it would be interesting to learn what others, who have seen the thrilling sight of a stooping falcon, have thought about its speed in flight. Such a sight must be rare indeed today, for not many of these noble birds are left at their immemorial eyries on the great cliffs of England. The peregrine falcon takes pigeons, and pigeons nowadays bring messages from wrecked aircraft, so the order has gone forth for its destruction.

June 7, 1943

The Trout Stream

Below the bottom of the garden the river ran, or rather moved sluggishly. The water was muddy, for the rivermen were above, pulling 'weed', as they called the green skeins of algae which grew from the shoals of sludge in the river. The sludge came into the river during rainy weather from the drains and culverts. It was an unhappy thing, for the occupant of the garden, to see the dirty water moving slowly past, while bubbles fizzled to the top. Those bubbles were of carbonic acid gas, and they meant death to the natural life of the river.

A polluted river dies slowly. A poisoned river dies swiftly; witness a certain lovely river in Kent, which died swiftly after the paper mills began to work at the beginning of this century. Once in summer that river was beautiful with mayfly and trout-ring, leaping dace and the dance of sedge and silverhorns at evening. The sedge and the silverhorn are two water flies. The sedge lives for a year as a crawling nymph in a little house made of stone and stick, cemented together by a secretion in the insect's jaws. It is known as a caddis. Pull a bine of water-weed from a living stream and you will find a caddis on it somewhere. After a year of underwater life, the caddis swims out as a nymph, its pellicle or skin splits, and a fly crawls forth. A brief aerial dance mating, and at evening it dips to drop its egg-clusters on the water, thus beginning anew the eternal cycle of life, which is also the sedge's ending, as, exhausted, it falls spent on the water. A slow ring, and a trout has taken it.

Silverhorns is a dusky little fly with antennae looking as though they have been touched with aluminium paint. It flies to and fro near the surface of the water, in its nuptial dance, so busily, for time is short: one short summer day, without drink or food, and its aerial life is ended.

When the paper mills began to pour their 'effluents' in, all life in the river died swiftly, for the water from the drains was poisonous. All that grew therein afterwards was the algae of decay – the lowest form of vegetable life, sullen and dispiriting.

A polluted river dies slowly. First the small invisible life, deprived of oxygen (which the sludge absorbs), ceases to exist, and the microscopic vegetable growths on which the nymphs live. The more delicate and ephemeral of the flies – olive dun, pale watery, iron blue, grannom and mayfly – slowly become extinct. Trout eggs, laid in autumn in the gravelly shallows, are attacked by fungus disease. Those which hatch find no food and die. Gradually, as more sludge pours into the river, a creeping paralysis of death spreads down its bed, once teeming with life. There comes a period in summer when the heat of the sun takes what little oxygen the water holds in solution from the air: the moment of lifelessness, of asphyxiation, suddenly arrives. Older trout, which hitherto have survived, thin and dark, turn on their sides, gape irregularly and drift downstream, bellies up. The coarser fish exist sluggishly; but in the end as the oxygen is absorbed by the silt of decay they, too, die away diseased. Last to remain are the eels, but even they must breathe; and when the water is entirely dead, acid and sour, they, too, are no more. Once a pure English stream, there remains now but an open drain – effect of slovenliness, the ignorance, and the selfishness of man.

I went to see the bottom of the garden, where my friend had tried to make a trout run. Gradually clearing the garden of stone and bits of broken brick and tile (for once a bullock yard had stood there) he had wheeled barrow-loads to the river and tipped them over the bank. Then with a rake he had spread them diagonally downstream, to form a slight barrier to the middle of the river-bed. This quickened the flow on the further side, and caused a pleasing ripple on the new shallows below the near bank. The flow or 'run' began to scour the mud under the further bank, and when at evening the water was running clear again, it was seen that a small channel had been cut, and the old gravelly bed of the river was exposed. The ripple water made a slight music and we watched a kingfisher flash by.

My friend told me that he almost could believe it to be an omen, for there had not been a kingfisher on the river for six years. The next day, going to the bank, I became aware of a brownish-purple movement in the water, and as my eyes became accustomed to the dance and swirl, I saw that many fish were moving just under the surface. A reddish-brown fin cut the water, and at once a dozen fish jostled after it, half out of water, making a splashing in the run. They were roach which were spawning there. They had found a clear area of gravel, and water en-livened by the ripple and flow, and had chosen the place to lay their eggs.

A female roach of about a foot in length was attended by half a dozen smaller males. The splashing was made as she turned on her side to flap in order to extrude the strings of jelly-like eggs. At once the male fish dashed forward to cover them with their milt. We stood still, and soon I saw that nearly a hundred fish were cruising about, or lying in the calmer water below the 'run'. And further downstream were half a dozen ducks, eagerly quapping the eggs in the water-weed where they had lodged!

June 14, 1943

The Story of Cheepy

While the metal wings and the thundering steel hearts are passing overhead in the summer sky, with great swift shadows flicking over the summer earth, let us pause a moment and regard this little thing on the garden path, which also has wings and a heart; but whose shadow is small and hesitant. From the vast power of the daylight bombers roaring through the sky, turn to the humble little chicken who is about to crouch beside the hot stone and drop its wings to shelter five smaller objects which run to it, with tiny cheeping cries. And while others tell the story of the beautiful bombs, let me tell the story of Cheepy, and the guinea-fowl chicks.

Cheepy was the name given by the children to a wet little creature that was found at the edge of a nettle patch near the farm buildings. How it got there it is not known. Perhaps it was one of a brood hatched by a hen that had laid away from the premises; but the mystery was, where was the hen and the other chicks, if this was so? Anyway, the lone chick was found shivering by the nettles, picked up, and taken home, to be put in a basket with bits of flannel in the kitchen hot-cupboard. The children peeped at it, held it for warmth in their hands, and watched with delight as its eyes closed sleeping, and it uttered faint sounds of happiness. They called it Cheepy.

After a couple of days Cheepy was running about happily over the kitchen floor, and by the fourth day had found its way into the parlour and was used to sitting on one of the small boys' laps. There were kittens on the floor, too, and a young wood owl called Hooly who liked to sleep among the hats and gloves ranged on the lower half of the oak and mahogany tallboy (but that, as Kipling says, is another story). Cheepy showed no fear, and why, indeed, should it, for they were all friends together. Even the mother cat did not object when Cheepy perched on her head one day and went to sleep.

When Cheepy was ten days old, and its feathers were beginning to sprout from soft grey quills, five guinea-fowl eggs hatched in the

incubator, and soon five small chicks were squatting in the basket in the hot-cupboard. They fed with Cheepy, and to our astonishment the chick was to be seen leading them on the garden bed by the path outside the farmhouse door, scratching for them, and when they ran to her for shelter she dropped her minute wing-stubs and was immediately a little hen. She had adopted them.

She led them into the kitchen at evening time, and they all got into the basket. Down below, in the basement, so to speak, two other families lived, occupying two baskets. In one were four kittens, sons and daughters of a tortoiseshell cat; in the other, another quartette of kittens, belonging to a rough rat-eating cat named Eric. At least, Eric had been rough until her first kittens arrived, when her fierce eyes became meditative and she who was almost untouchable before – liable to bite if stroked in the wrong place – became pliable and acquiescent.

Every day Eric looked in at the other basket to see how her friend's little lot were getting on. This little lot were smaller than her own, having been born about two weeks later. Once one of Eric's kittens was put in the other basket; after sniffing and hesitating, she took it back to her own basket.

The days went on, the chicks grew in size and speed, the kittens learned to climb out of their baskets and explore the cupboard and the tiled floor of the kitchen, while the mother cats learned to appreciate the blessings of tranquillity a few yards away from their offspring, and, if possible, from an unscaleable higher level. Gold-finches nested in the apple trees, starlings and jackdaws in the walnut in the middle of the garden, robins in a bank (second brood) and also wrens, a pipit, a treecreeper and, blessed sight after six years' absence, a pair of kingfishers not far off in a hole in a bank.

The farmhouse was near the road, and often in the walls could be heard the rolling trundle of steel tracks and the deeper hum of rubber tyres; a dangerous place, though quiet in comparison with the incessant passing of peace-time summer traffic.

One afternoon Cheepy and her family were dusting themselves in the path worn by many boots leaving the farmhouse door, where was fine dust, glinting in the sun. The tortoiseshell cat sat near, waiting for her especial friend, a boy who was her owner – ownership in this case meaning a lavishment of affection in terms of crooning talk and much smoothing of soft hair. Soon would be time of coming home from school, and the cat was usually there to greet her friend.

A rough old shaggy dog looked round the corner, stared at the chicks, and went forward as if to satisfy its curiosity. Dogs are inquisitive creatures, always on the look-out for something interesting. Perhaps it found the sight of so small a hen, only partly covered with feathers, a matter for investigation, without the least intention of interfering, of course. Just a slight and momentary curiosity.

But the cat thought he meant harm, for she ran forward and tapped him on the side of the nose. With a stifled cry, more of injured innocence than pain, the shaggy old dog turned tail and trotted away. The cat sat at the edge of the road, flicking its tail.

She watched Cheepy and her brood crossing the road, which lay between two walls, very narrow, much rolled by rubber tyres. Suddenly there was a squeal of brakes, and large tyres slowed down; the cat ran forward to the scattered chicks, which ran all ways; and when the shadow of the lorry had passed, there she lay, with teeth showing, and glazed eyes, beside the feebly kicking Cheepy.

When the boy heard he was inconsolable, moving quietly about the garden and the house, with a pale face. It was the first time he had realised Death. Cheepy and Torty, the cat, were buried in the garden, and some seeds sown over their grave; while in the kitchen, as the bombers roll in thunder through the night, the remaining cat lies contentedly on the mat, eight kittens and five guinea-fowl chicks snuggled against her.

June 21, 1943

Peace in War

My colleague Mr Jacob Tonson,* whose place I am taking in these Monday articles for a while, remarked in one of his articles how war turns things topsy-turvy, or words to that effect. When I read his list of paradoxes I thought of one instance on my farm, of how a small sample of weed-seed (charlock, or carlick as they call it in Norfolk) was declared by the buyer to be 'spoiled' by a few barley kernels ... and how it paid me, as a farmer, to put the carlick through the dressing machine and so remove the corn seeds which spoiled the pure weed-seeds.

The reason is that some cage-birds thrive on the small, round, oily seed of carlick, while the barley might stick in their throats and choke them. And the price of carlick seed, that curse of good husbandry? I got 64s. a cwt., but later on the price rose to £110 a ton!

Thus the farmer with land full of 'rubbish', the slobberer of the pre-war period, was in a position to make a small fortune out of weeds, if he felt that way about things. The good farmer would, in my experience, rather have good, true crops and a moderate profit than receive a fantastic price for his wretched weeds.

The majority of farmers are good men; black markets don't start in the country, nor do international wars. Wars are a disease of the gold of the towns and cities, of pavements and offices, not of green fields and pastures.

These reflections arise in part because I have been looking at Major Edward Seago's new book, called *Peace in War*†. It contains about two dozen pictures which the artist has painted during rare periods of leave from the Army, in which he now serves as a Camouflage Officer. Each picture in the book is accompanied by a chapter describing how it was painted. At the beginning of the book the author-artist wins our sympathy by the modesty of his *credo*:

*Henry Williamson reverted to writing under his own name from June 21.
†Published by Collins at 12s 6d. in 1943.

39

There is a certain grandeur in the wide stretches of East Anglia, and
a strange subtlety of constant change, which has inspired some of the
greatest English landscapes. Each mood has a beauty of its own,
whether in repose or raked by the sharp east wind. In the happy
painting ground of Cotman, Crome and Constable, I am making no
more than a modest attempt to follow in the tradition of the English
school, which they endowed with such brilliance and harmony...
I have only a simple perception, but the country is full of simple things
of real beauty, and many of them may pass unnoticed by those more
out of touch with a simple life.

This is Edward Seago's belief and purpose, and with a quiet zest he
sets out during various leaves with paint box and brushes and palette,
and often a rug to keep him warm from the sharp east wind, to paint
what he sees and loves. I have watched him on the uplands of my
farm, huddled on a stool, painting for hour after hour. I have met him
on the coast road coming from Morston Church, in the wintry
twilight, lamenting in his quiet voice that the sky-tints are changing
so rapidly, and each so marvellous, that almost by force he had to be
brought home to drink tea and afterwards to smoke his pipe in my
'studio' (where I am writing these notes) and talk about his beloved
North Norfolk coast.

'Studio' is perhaps a pretentious word for this shell of an old
smallholder's barn, with open hearth of bricks and made up with the
aid of builders' oddments bought at various auctions before the war.
Someone in the family, or perhaps a visitor, called it 'a studio', and
the name has remained, and it is too late now to change it. Writing-
room it was supposed to have been; a place where the business of
the farm would not obtrude. Yet all around me are paint pots and
hammers, nails, hoes, an axe, coils of rope, old sacks – ranged tidily,
yet still an obtrusion. No escape in the 'studio' from the farm; no
Jekyll and Hyde business, no complete metamorphosis from field
worker to literary gent. It was intended as a sanctuary, in the days of
toiling to reconstruct cottage and buildings and to reclaim weedy
acres; the word 'studio' held the promise of peace and reflection, so
essential for literary creation, an escape from oil-grained hands and
broken nails, from chaff-dust in nostrils and hair and worn-out
overalls... Well, that is life, and here I am writing in the 'studio',
which is full of books seldom looked at, of hanging bunches of
tobacco leaves seldom smoked, a deep leather armchair seldom sat in.
There have been moments, however, as in that day when Ted Seago

walked in, and we sat before the fire of 'great old bull-thorns', and talked about a better England arising beyond the serrated horizon of war. I remember we discussed this very book, to be called *Peace in War*, to be a record of his escapes into the world of colour and form and line. Which is not to say that the good artist cannot also be the good soldier. Here is Edward Seago:

> . . . the English countryside is threatened; a shield must protect it. The day will come once more . . . when the shield is lowered from the face of the land.

There is his belief, quite simple, entirely firm; the simple artist is also the simple Englishman doing his duty.

In one of the pictures a figure lolls across an armchair in a cottage room. A cup of tea is on the table, a book in the figure's hands. The picture is called Moat Cottage. I know that room, that chair, that figure of a young man relaxed after his flying duties. The Moat Cottage is near a river in which trout rise in steady rings in the summer evening twilight. A few miles away is the air station. The figure is that of 'Crasher', to whom the book is dedicated, with this quotation from the poem by Robert Bridges:

> O youth whose hope is high,
>   Who doth to Truth aspire;
> Whether thou live or die,
>   O look not back or tire.

Now, as I look at *Peace in War* in the quiet of the 'studio', I reflect how apt, how prophetic, were the four lines of poetry; for 'Crasher' did not look back, nor did he tire; but fell to death in his Spitfire on the day the book was published, a little over a fortnight ago.

June 28, 1943

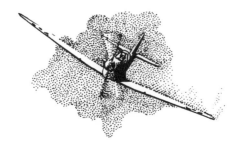

Hooly

I

Ben the gamekeeper, passing by the overgrown willows of the choked duck-decoy, saw an owl perched on a branch within a few feet of his face. 'It looked at me, but appeared to take no notice.' I asked him if he shot it. 'Certainly not. Owls do good. Look at the rats and mice they take in a night!'

Mr H. J. Massingham, the naturalist, who has written well about North Norfolk, and especially of the Blakeney marshes and the tern sanctuary of the Point, has referred bitterly to the 'shoot and stuff' attitude of the county. He was perhaps thinking of the days of his boyhood, when anything with a curved beak or a talon'd foot was knocked over in the interest of the pheasant. Now Norfolk, in my opinion, especially the north coastal district, is probably more like Old England than any other part of the island (or was until the war began to 'liven things up a bit'), and this has its advantages as well as its disadvantages; but, generally speaking, I should say that the 'shoot and stuff' attitude has gone. I knew before I spoke that the question to Ben was unnecessary, for Ben is sensible and obliging, and if he knows that owls and kestrels are especially regarded on this farm, he would be the last to raise that booming double-barrel which at times is to be heard in the woods, as with his son he helps to obliterate the chiselling rabbit.

The owl that Ben saw on the willow branch was, I like to think, a tame owl which we reared in the cottage. How it came to us was this way. One evening, coming in to supper, I saw a small object, looking like a lump of dough excessively covered with mildew, in a basket on the coconut mat of the kitchen floor. Richard, the youngest, explained that it was 'lost', and had been brought to the door 'by a little old boy'. Apparently this 'little old boy', aged about five years, had found the object under a tree in the lane. It could not have been lost very long,

43

for it was warm and comfortably covered with flesh. It had a long, thin head and a beak which tried to swallow my finger when I knelt down to stroke it. It chirruped, and was hungry.

There was an air-rifle in the cupboard, and some sparrows on the roof. Not long afterwards one of those sparrows went, piece by piece, into the owlet's crop. When I went back for more, the sparrows, in a row on the ridge-tile, took immediate evasive action into the unseen road below. Thereafter they were never about more than half a second after the barrel of the rifle had appeared, though many a small silvery mark was left on the ridge just after their legs and tail-feathers had vanished from view. 'Huh, wise guys,' said another of the innumerable small boys that haunt our house, watching one such failure. He waited with a catapult round the gateway, but the piece of chalk flipped from his feeble engine sped even more harmlessly through the air.

Thereafter Hooly, as the owlet was called, had to be fed on the flesh and fur of young rabbits. It was my job to procure these little animals. After working and scheming all day (for literary work and farming together require a lot of scheming) I was bored with the idea of having to go out every night to effect the mortification of some miserable little scurrying quadruped. However, duty had to be done; and usually in the late twilight as the cup of tea was cooling on the table, I wandered in with my object of the chase, to be greeted, as the days lengthened into midsummer, and the bombers began to roar in the sky, by the invariable sight of a small monkey-like object apparently doing a tight-rope act on the ridge, and flapping down the tiles to jump on my shoulder and scream for sections of the mortified quadruped.

By this time Hooly had explored the lower parts of the cottage and was used to sleeping on the tallboy, among the caps and gloves laid out there in an orderly manner (at what cost in a family of four boys, only one entitled to the old school tie, I leave it to literary biography to decide). Hooly flapped and hauled his way to the tallboy when he felt sleepy, and, shooting his legs out behind him like a tired spaniel on hot summer sands, closed his eyes and slumbered. Sometimes he played with a green and red glove, relic of peace-time skiing in the snows of New England; in play he was a feathered kitten, throwing up the glove and catching it with his beak. He was a nice little owl, and only once tried to swallow my ear-lobe while I was a bit procrastinating with his rabbit.

Hooly wandered about the roof, and lost the habit of putting himself to bed in his little basket. (From the first he had slept happily in the hot cupboard.) He was a wild-looking bird, with large eyes dark as grapes with the bloom on them, and his fearlessness was an endearing thing. He had never shown fear, but had accepted us all with almost human naturalness. As a fledgeling, crouching in his basket with head bowed in sleep, he had merely chirruped when a slender boyish finger had scratched near his large ear cavities. He had not raised his head with alarm, but accepted the caress in the spirit in which it was offered.

One night, as I was standing immobile on the garden path, looking at Hooly on the ridge tiles of the roof, a strange owl flew a few feet over my head and braked with its wide, soft wings. Seeing the apparition, Hooly snapped his beak in alarm. At the same moment the owl lit on the roof beside him, and turned its head to take in any movement – the quick glance of a wild creature, whose life is one calculation in motion after another. The glance was of a second's duration before the bird turned to Hooly, revealing that it carried a sparrow in its beak. With a swift movement the sparrow was transferred to a foot. With sideway striking motion Hooly snatched it. The old bird flapped up and away. Hooly stood there, the dead sparrow in his foot. He took the best part of half an hour to break it up with pluckings and pullings; first one wing was swallowed, then another, and at last the skull was gulped down. Thereafter he walked and flapped to the chimney stack, and settled down for a rest; the evening star shone brighter in the sky, and I went to bed.

July 5, 1943

II

We left Hooly, the young tame tawny owl, settled among the farmhouse chimney pots to sleep, content with his meal of a sparrow. What was the strange owl that brought him the sparrow, we asked ourselves. Was it his mother or father, if so, why did Hooly snap his beak in fear when the big dark wings approached? Had Hooly's mother known all along that her nestling was in the kitchen? Had she heard him chirruping at night, and with the natural fidelity of most birds waited and watched for her little one?

The next night Hooly was on his roof when the old bird came again, this time with a young rat. Hooly thereupon dropped the stale rabbit pelt he was playing with and retired with the rat to the chimney stack. Soon afterwards the tail of the rat was sticking out of his mouth like a cigar as he huddled himself besides the pale yellow and red pots. During the following day he was missing, but at evening time, as the sun was sinking, we heard his chissiking cries, and I went over to the tall trees behind the wooden Institute hut and he saw me and flew down and sat on my shoulder. I walked across the road and fed him by the draw-well cover. As soon as he was fed he flew up to the roof and climbed and flapped to his favourite ridge.

The next evening when I called him he sailed on broad brown wings over the Institute roof to my shoulder. Two soldiers passed, walking up and down the village street to find something interesting, but they took no notice of an owl flying to a man's shoulder. Perhaps they were townsmen and saw nothing unusual in such a sight; perhaps they were hurrying to find the fish and chips hut. Perhaps Hooly looked like a cat on my shoulder; perhaps they didn't like our two faces . . .

Those tall green trees of sycamore and ash became the owlet's day hide and roost. Every evening I called him; every evening he flew and glided to my shoulder; but one night he was missing.

It was a Friday night. I knew it was Friday by the smell of fish and chips wafted on the western breeze from the middle of the village. No Hooly on Saturday. On the Sunday morning I was awakened by a screaking in my bedroom, and there was a strained oval face on the window-sill, staring with misery in its eyes, a shrill anguish in its thin cries, its feet shifting as with pain. Seeing a grey woollen sock on the chair, the owl flew to it, and standing on it made a hopeless attempt to swallow it.

It was 5 o'clock, it was Sunday, it was the day of rest; but no one could relax while those famished eyes stared so sharply; and getting out of bed I put on dressing gown and slippers to get his rabbit. But a cat had apparently taken it during the night, from where I had hung it on the outer brick casing of the draw-well. Meanwhile Hooly was facing me, dancing like a dervish, screeching like an engine bearing about to seize. I went to the larder, but found only some bacon and the remains of a potato pasty.

Sunday, the day of rest; no matter, the truant must be fed. Ah, the air-rifle, and a sparrow! But the sparrows, those wise guys, were absent. Perhaps they were organised as a sort of avian Home Guard; for when I returned round the corner to the well, to find Hooly, there were a dozen or more of them around him, chattering, and one old cock was actually pulling a feather from the back of his head. Seeing me, they scattered and skulked in the lilac bushes, while the air-rifle phutted in vain.

I went down to the farm and waited in the chalk quarry below the beech trees. Sparrows chirped in their nests under the tiles of the cart-shed, but I would not take a fledgeling direct from its nest. Then a starling flew to a branch of an ash tree, and fell dead as the little waisted pellet of lead spun through its chest. Starlings were rank-tasting, I suspected, as the hawks and owls I kept as a boy never ate them; but Hooly found this one nicer than a woollen sock.

Thereafter he took to being absent at twilight and came instead to my window at dawn, crying and flapping for food and walking over the blanket to yell in my ear if I did not awake. Sometimes he visited other cottage windows, and from one in particular I saw him leaving hurriedly, accompanied by oaths and the slamming of the window. Unfortunately, other people in the village had been trying to feed Hooly, or rather had tried to get him to take pieces of bread, and so his singleness of mind had disintegrated, and he went to anyone and to any open window. Robert, one of the boys, once woke up and found Hooly pulling his hair. Our boys liked Hooly, of course, and welcomed him at any hour of the day or night; but not so all of the neighbours.

When Hooly disappeared I thought someone must have shot him, but he returned after a few evenings, flying down to the top bar of the draw-well. He screaked down at my face, but when I offered my shoulder he edged away. Obviously someone had tried to handle him instead of letting him perch free on wrist or shoulder.

While he perched there nine swallows, with ringing cries, began to ring above and around the circular brick well. First one, then another, 'peeled off' and dived at him, swishing by within an inch of his amazed and jerky eyes, to zoom and join again the ring above. One after another they came down, sweeping up again and taking their turn to dive once more. They cut at him from in front and behind, and Hooly did not like it. He flew away. It was then that I heard another owl call, and turning I saw it perching on the chimney rim of my studio stack.

That, then, was the secret! The wild owl was hunting for and feeding Hooly. The next night the two birds came, and while the old bird perched in a damson tree, Hooly flew down to my shoulder. He came by habit; he cried to me by habit, although he was not really hungry. He came because of what a scientist would call an association of ideas; but what I would call friendship. The old owl had accepted the fact that Hooly had human friends and waited quietly until he was ready to fly off again.

About a week later we heard that an owl had been shot in a neighbouring village for 'attacking soldiers'. Was this the end of our little tame bird that had never known fear of anyone?

I dreaded so; but the very next evening down by the duckpond, I saw him perched on a willow branch. He allowed me to stroke his head while his eyes closed; just like a cat, he liked being scratched about the ears. Hooly looked very handsome in his (or her) new browns and blacks and whites, and the eyes had that full and authentic keenness of perfect natural form. 'Hooly,' I said, 'Hooly.' He (or she) gave me a long stare; a baby chirrup came from the beak; then, without a cry, Hooly flew into the twilight after a dark, silent-winged form; and so he flew out of our lives. And if you remember the beginning of this little history of an owl, you will recall that Ben the keeper, passing the duck decoy the other day, saw an owl on a branch and passed by it as near as you pass a man on the pavement, and the owl was quite easy about it. So was Ben, and so am I, for I feel sure it was our Hooly.

July 12, 1943

Of Men and Books

Visiting Henry Williamson in Cromer hospital (where he is now progressing satisfactorily after an operation)* I learned the good news that Faber & Faber are shortly publishing Miss Lilias Rider Haggard's *Norfolk Life*. Many readers of 'The Countrywoman's' Monday articles will be glad to learn that a selection of them is being printed in book form under this title. Henry Williamson is the editor, for Miss Haggard found that, with the coming of the war, her numerous duties were soon multiplied. I looked into a page-proof set which lay on the table beside Williamson's bed, which he said, had just been returned by A. J. Munnings, the artist, now living at Withypool, in Somerset – a few miles away from the moorland home of Williamson in Devon. Munnings was enthusiastic, declaring that the book was first class. It takes much patience and tenacity to chronicle the details and little happenings of everyday life; their record often seems exasperatingly trivial to the writer; but seen in retrospect, how the authenticity of such 'small beer' brings life to the page! Perhaps the most outstanding example of patient, everyday writing is to be found in Pepys' *Diaries* – now among the most interesting in the world.

More literary news – Adrian Bell, author of the fascinating farming autobiography beginning with *Corduroy*, has bought some semi-derelict Suffolk land, which the W.A.C.† had actually taken over a

*This was written under Henry Williamson's previous *nom de plume* of 'Jacob Tonson'. Doubtless he felt that he could hardly review under his own name a book which he himself had edited. The operation was an appendectomy.

†War Agricultural Committee. These were county-based committees with legal powers to enforce full and efficient use of all land suitable for agriculture, which included the powers to direct farmers and landowners to plow up and crop their land, and even to requisition and supervise land themselves under the Defence Regulations. They also had the facilities to supply services of labour, machinery etc., which were necessary to comply with their directions, but which farmers could not always provide for themselves. The W.A.C. graded farms, and it says much for Williamson's efforts and farming methods that the derelict farm he took over in 1937 was consistently graded an 'A' farm.

week before Adrian Bell bought the land. So the success of Bell's latest book – *Apple Acre* – has resulted in the author acquiring the title to 'Eighty-seven Acres of England'. As Bell wrote to his friend Williamson:

> I took on everything lock, stock and barrel, and am gradually weeding out. It is a task which takes all my time, as you can imagine, but it will, I think, be worth it. It appeals to me to turn 87 acres of England into what 87 acres of England ought to be. . . . When I took over the farm there were only three acres of corn of any kind, and most of the land was still unplowed (late spring), so I shan't have a bumper harvest this year. The top layer of soil had grown so thin through progressive shallow plowing for many years, that there was hardly any live soil left at all. Now acres of yellow foot-deep fallows lie baking in the July sun.

Well, Adrian Bell has a job before him, beginning at a time when labour and implements are almost unobtainable. What the 'lock, stock and barrel' of a 'C' farm were like we can only imagine.

July 19, 1943

The Tragic Spirit

I

Some listeners to the BBC programmes must have hesitated on a Monday evening in mid-July, 1943, after the news of the battles in Sicily and Russia – the dreaded two-front war of Adolf Hitler – between listening to Mr J. B. Priestley speaking on the Home Front, and Mr Noel Coward singing and reciting his own works on the Forces wavelength.

Mr Priestley was presented to Home listeners as plain Mr Priestley; but Mr Coward was welcomed to the Forces as a national figure. As the hook-up in the hospital in which I was lying was for the Forces only, I had no alternative, and I listened to Mr Coward with hopeful attention.

After the songs, rendered in Mr Coward's careful tones, we were given a recitation about bombers passing in the night, and the feelings their engine noises aroused in the civilian hearing them in the darkness of his house below. Those noises are torrential.

I have lived for some years near a Devon river, and when the south-west Atlantic gale blew the heavy rains across Exmoor, the river rose many feet in a few hours and the undulating waters roared down the valley, surging over the weirs and falling with a tremendous noise; but the passing of a thousand and more heavy bombers in the Norfolk night air is like the final scene in Götterdämmerung itself.

Mr Coward is always topical. From the frustrations and inanities of the early 'twenties, the anti-war bitterness of the later 'twenties, or the reproduction of the old masters of the Vienna waltzes and the Kiplingesque fervours of *Cavalcade* to the present war for freedom and civilisation, Mr Coward collects all the urban moods. Mr Coward is a national figure.

The verses were arresting; a tribute of safe middle age to perilous youth. They were not pure tribute, however; there was a disparaging comparison of aircraft crews with 'reserved musicians' and with 'soft, hysterical actors.' I wondered what was in Mr Coward's mind when he wrote the verses; and if he would have felt like that had he been one of the crew of an aircraft or battleship, or in an infantry platoon; of course he wouldn't, nor would the feelings that contributed to his next song have survived an apprenticeship, however brief, in real action – as opposed to action in a film studio. It was essentially a middle-aged civilian's song, a satire which young men in uniform will soon be singing as a mess room joke – 'Don't let's be beastly to the Germans!' Perhaps, however, I am prejudiced; this may be the work of a great poet, perhaps the war poet, which this war so far is said not to have produced. Or is Lord Vansittart, who also writes verses, the chosen one?

But as a judge of civilian war poets, or poetasters, I am prejudiced. I do not like civilians who 'kill Germans with their mouths.' This prejudice derives from the ancient battlefields of Somme and Ypres, whereon soldiers generally were adamant to the utterances and writings of the national figures of those faraway days.

I recall the incident of a celebrated author and journalist later knighted, giving a lecture at Corps Headquarters to the remnants of a division which had survived Hulloch and the Hohenzollern Redoubt, and was withdrawn to rest. The subject of the lecture was the battle of Loos. The lecturer, the famous newspaper correspondent, was a sensitive fellow, and probably he gave the lecture at the request of the divisional commander, who might have been an admirer of his pre-war novels.

After the lecture questions were invited. An old colonel arose. 'I would like to ask just one question,' he said. 'The other day I fought with my battalion in the battle of Loos. Now, having listened carefully to all that has been said, I am convinced that I was never there. Can the lecturer explain that, please?'

It was a bitter and embarrassing thing to do; but the chasm between the worlds of those who went through the mud and the blood, and those who talked and wrote and lectured and preached in heroic or sentimental vein about the war, was too wide. The civilians' truth was not the soldiers'.

There was a national figure called Horatio Bottomley making grand speeches which surely would have earned him a KBE if he had not been also too elusive a financier; and on the other side there was General Ludendorff at Tannenburg, in East Prussia, thanking God for His goodness to the Fatherland.

Among the smaller fry, singing their songs of hate and derision, were such figures as those painted by Mr C.R.W. Nevinson – called 'Broadway Patriots', singing perhaps, 'For sure the Kaiser likes the dear old tanks.'

In contrast to these lath and plaster heroics were the young men whose minds and bodies suffered the clash of war,

> Whose world is but the trembling of a flare,
> And heaven but as the highway for a shell.

July 26, 1943

II

Many men, many minds. Under each gravestone a world lies buried. Whose world, then, shall it be? My world is prejudiced, I am unable to alter myself (and I have tried); my world is the world of soldiers of Somme and Ypres and Siegfried Stellung. Has that old world any links with the soldiers' world of today? Often I wonder, but without certitude. Does history repeat itself? We know that people change; perhaps that is why history is said to repeat itself.

People change. Who would have thought in 1918 that a discredited and pacifist member of Parliament, who had been expelled from a local golf club for his supposed traitorous attitude to his country at war, whose meetings were broken up by roughs hired by that national figure, Mr Horatio Bottomley, would in less than six years become the idol of the populace, the very populace which had forgotten by then that once it had said that he ought to be put up against a wall and shot, but which made him Prime Minister instead?*

People change, but there is at least one historical instance of a man being true to himself. In history there is a Figure greater than that of any national proportions, around whom many thousands had pressed, multitudes which in a few short weeks were crying for His death, to the distress of the Roman governor who had begged the silent Figure to make some defence, and thereby perchance enable the governor, who obviously recognised Truth when he saw it, to save innocence from the propagated fury of the mob.

Moods of human beings change. The pendulum of a generation

*Ramsay MacDonald.

swings from left to right, from right to left again. The pacifist becomes the supporter of a war; the hysterical anti-war author becomes the jingo patriot; the slacker of 1914–18 becomes righteously imbued with spy-mania in 1940. These phenomena are merely obverse aspects of the same character. There is no tragedy or even irony in this, for the change or alteration is only superficial. These characters, whether of parochial or national size, are soon forgotten.

It is when men of authentic genius change that the spirit of Man is wounded, when they cease to 'fulfil the law and the prophets,' and become a law unto themselves; when the still small voice becomes a shout, when the gift of clairvoyance is transmitted into the sword-flash, and thereafter the bright star burns sultry, then black. In my lifetime I have known such a tragedy.

> So all had been in vain. In vain the sacrifices and privations, in vain the hunger and thirst for endless months, in vain those hours when the fear of death gripped our souls, and in vain the deaths of two millions who fell in the fulfilment of their duty. . . . Was it for this that the volunteer regiments followed the old comrades in the autumn of the same year? Was it for this that those boys of 17 years of age mingled with the soil of Flanders? Did all this happen so that a gang of despicable criminals might lay their hands on the Fatherland?

I know that Flanders soil, for the English battalion in which I served as a 17-year-old volunteer clashed 'in the autumn of the same year' with the very battalion in which the author of the preceding quotation was serving as a private soldier. His genius or clairvoyance led him later to the highest place in the respect and love of millions of youths, but in that high place he forgot the authentic truth of the battlefields, which is never found among the plausible and cunning of the market place. So beset, the old soldier could no longer trust himself, the old soldier could not truly endure. History will endorse what he wrote of others in 1919 to be his own indictment twenty years later.

August 2, 1943

Answers to Correspondents

W hat a responsibility an editor has, to be sure! The other day, following on an announcement in this newspaper that Miss Lilias Rider Haggard's *Norfolk Life*, edited by myself, was shortly being published by Messrs Faber, I received a letter which filled me with apprehension. Perhaps I ought to say first that, when making up the book from several years' notes and articles of 'The Countrywoman', my chief difficulty was that of selecting about 70,000 words (the average length of a book) from nearly three times that number. Therefore much good stuff had to be omitted. Now what will my Fakenham correspondent think of me, as an editor, if a favourite passage of his has been omitted? But let him speak for himself:

> I trust your discerning eye may be wide-open against any possibility of the omission of the paragraph describing 'The Countrywoman's' brief but all-sufficient experience of looking after chickens. She was exasperated by them to the superbly exact description that: 'FOR LOW CUNNING AND UTTER IDIOCY chickens are the most exasperating of domestic animals.'
>
> Listening to the plaints of my poultry-keeping friends, I have often quoted those words to them, and have been asked 'to write them words down for me, so I kin remember 'em.' I know of one large chicken house where 'low cunning and utter idiocy' is scrawled on the freshest surfaced plank of its interior, to serve as a soothing substitute for a pent-up torrent of words unrefined and highly explosive. Now in periods of extreme annoyance my poultry friend just glances at *five words only* and calmly says, 'Just what you are, you beauties!' Thus has 'The Countrywoman' brought the comfort of a concentrated essence of expression to an exasperated poultry-keeper.

Well, I was beginning to think that my acts in the Norfolk air were perhaps peculiar; but I find I have some way to go yet before I take to writing up slogans for the livestock on my little farm. Certainly I tried the effect of slogans for human beings, such as that in the hovel or 'cart-shud':

DANGER OF FIRE

NO SMOKING

but soon 'the foreigner' had to learn that this, with other requests for tidiness and order, was a direct attack on the liberty of the subject. For a little while a miniature world-war was carried on about these 'bad lands', an ideological conflict between the principle of Smoke or Not to Smoke in Haybarns and Stables, Plow-breasts to be Greased after Use or to be Left to Rust, Corn-sacks to be Hung Up after Use or Left for Rats to Gnaw, Dead Rats to be Buried or to become Hosts for Blowflies, etc. Local tradition with the irrefutable argument that No One Else About Here Does It. If Waterloo was won on the playing fields of Eton, I sometimes think, with the megalomania of loneliness, that Dunkirk and Singapore were lost on my farm.

Another correspondent applies for work on the aforesaid 'bad lands'. He states, with admirable simplicity, that he will be content with a cottage and a wage of £3 or £4 a week, with some rough shooting, and time off occasionally to explore local historical monuments. He adds that he has no previous farming experience, but that he is most keen to get out of his present job. He doesn't enclose a stamped addressed envelope, and he suggests that I go to call on him when next I am in London. He adds that having read *The Story of a Norfolk Farm*, he has developed the urge to 'tickle the old earth with a pitchfork.'

Now, while I appreciate his spirit at its proper worth, I hardly know what, or how, to reply. Memory serves to tell me that these 'bad lands' have experienced some 'earth-ticklers' before. Between Intellectualism and Low Cunning and Utter Idiocy the farmer stands, faced with a Two-Front War. Perhaps to see the farm at its best one should visit it on a threshing day, when the little permanent staff is, of necessity, augmented by amateur helpers. Every half-hour or so the amateurs descend for a smoke. Once, to hasten things up a bit (for we like to thresh at least seven or eight coombs an hour) help was given to the flaccid amateurs on the stack; and soon so many boots were pressing the sheaves that they almost became silage. At the end of the day we had threshed fifty-five coombs. I am told that the local record is three hundred coombs in a day. Still, we have at least one record; once we threshed a stack of oats near a wood and got over five coombs of mice through the drum. Can any farmer beat that? Twenty bushels of mixed mice, finest Catsmeat Sample! Thousands more mice were not threshed out; they leapt about the stack, ran up the girls' legs, and poured over the eaves in grey masses. So numerous were they that the rats had been 'druv away'. I estimated 250 coombs of oats in the stack in August; we threshed out 110 only. And in case anyone writes in to say that I am a 'Z' farmer, and should be expelled from Neatest Norfolk, let me hasten to add that I had arranged for the stack to be threshed in early October of that terrible year of 1941, before the rains should come and make the approach along the waterside strip of grass impassable by the 17-ton engine and box; but for reasons which need not be remembered now, it didn't happen until the following March. Meanwhile, several hundred thousand evacuee mice had been enjoying life at our expense. In the sombre yards the cattle, deprived of winter feed, were a dreadful sight; gaunt hips, and ringworm on staring coats. The Japanese swarmed over Malaya and Java and the mice swarmed over my oatstack; Singapore fell, it seemed to me, first in England. However, the real test of life is not to get bitter.

And, in another sense, not to get bit. I confess I have been bitten quite often. About two dozen people, in one way and another, and somehow, got themselves on or into this little holding, at one time or another during the past six years; and nearly all discovered that life was but getting out of the frying-pan into the fire. Not all, one or two did good work. But to return to my correspondent, who wants time off to explore Local Ruins, and a cottage (not one in a row, he explains) and help with his literary work and a bit of shooting, etc., I really feel this farm is not the place for him. There's no Music While You Work here; and the only literature is the faded slogans; and I feel somehow that he will not care for them.

August 9, 1943

On Children

Rosemary, a sporting young woman of nine years of age, recently wrote asking if I knew of a spare rabbit hutch on my farm, as she had a spare rabbit. I replied, truthfully, that I had a hutch, but no spare rabbit, and did she know of one? While mutual acquisitive negotiations were in progress, the following came to hand, as they say:

> My request to you for a spare hutch is now obsolete, as my rabbit has now died of pot-belly, due to eating Mr. ——'s spare cabbages. My rabbit did not have such a good live [sic] as Charles' Dutch mouse, which he bought at Gamage's for sixpence last holiday. Samuel (the mouse) fared well until Charles had to go back to school. Bitter tears, but Mummy suggested he should let it go and Samuel would be quite happy on the Common. Charles sobbed, 'Yes, but look at all the snakes on the Common, Samuel is sure to be attacked by one, and he has no means of defending himself,' so Charles put Samuel's cage in the toolshed and left the door open, with food there for him every day. The moment his gate was opened and he started exploring the shed, a little garden mouse appeared and they seemed to like each other. Samuel and wife go back to sleep in the cage every night, and a family of Free Dutch Allied mice are expected any moment.
>
> Charles is a keen fisherman, and spends every spare moment at school fishing. The other day he caught a 9-inch perch and sold it to a Monitor for 2s. 6d. He sent 2s. 6d. to a little fishing shop in Newbury with a polite note asking for some hooks – he got 18.

Two shillings and sixpence seems a good price for a Monitor in a preparatory school to pay for a bony perch; but perhaps in his spare time that Monitor was working on an aerodrome.*

The care that Charles showed for his mouse, and the imagination that revealed the terrifying defencelessness of a small rodent con-

---

*A wry reference to the inflated wages being paid at that time to labourers working on the many airfields being carved out of East Anglia's flat agricultural land. Farmers could not compete with these wages and many workers left the land.

fronted with a snake obviously reveals 'enlarged and numerous senses', which was the Blakeian prescription for the poetic mind. For such there are blanks in life even when memories of fish caught (and sold) and mice successfully launched into the marriage market are not sufficient. Charles wrote a poem in one of those blank moods:

> On a Saturday night I went for a stroll,
> Not a sound came near except a harsh flat bell toll –
> But O, worst of all, no one to talk to.

> I felt afraid, no words, no song,
> Except a dreadful harsh flat bell dong
> And O, worst of all, no one to talk to.

To the Charleses of the world one can say that it is not an awfully good time just now, and many others besides him feel just like that, off and on; but let us look forward to a time when the flat bell dongs are chased away by the bells pealing all over the land, bringing back Merrie England under the banner of Saint George, and all that such a banner should mean. It won't come about, in this world, without terrific working ability on the part of everyone, in and of village, town, city, parish, district, county. One for all, and all for one, Charles – as in the Eighth Army today, or the Navy or the R.A.F. Listen to what General Montgomery said a few weeks ago: 'The British soldier responds to leadership very easily. He is a very easy person to lead, and he is willing to be led. But I will say this about him, that if he is not well led he can be terribly bad.'

I went the other day to watch children at the village school recite, dance and sing. A great change has come over this school since first I knew it six years ago. It was a shabby village then; I used to feel, most of the time, like Charles in his poem. There was little or no village spirit. How could there be? There was neither the old spirit, when under the dominating personality of 'the ould Karnel' (Colonel) no man who was without work need want for work; nor was there any new spirit to take the place of that which had entirely decayed in the agricultural depression. The old order had gone, and nothing had taken its place. People had got along anyhow, for they had not a real chance to bring the best in them to the fore. And this showed itself in many ways; and one of the ways was in the aspect of the children. 1919–1939 – one of the worst periods in the history of England.

Today there is a change. The children look happy, and are free from mental fear and from those cloying repressions which reveal themselves in ragged speech and manners. A child's mind is a new thing; it can be made or marred by its environment. It is eager for the truth, and recognises it at once . . . the simple truth of the child's world. Its potential faith and belief are enormous. Leadership is the key to all education; and the school is fortunate in having one whose talent is obviously fitted to her task.

The essence of leadership is truth. The truth is never dull; it is the very light of life. The truth of a butterfly's colours, of an owl's sight in darkness, of why a bee visits a blossom, of why London is a port, of why the tides come in far over the marsh when the moon is full; even the truth of arithmetic, which (to give a simple example) saves counting thousands of pennies by changing them into shillings and pounds. The child's enormous curiosity *led* to the vision or recognition of such interesting things, does the rest. How different from the old pedagogic reiteration of the dust of things, often with a stick, things devoid of their life or spirit, crammed into the resisting and bored minds, as though children in school were chickens in one of those foul cramming batteries where the wretched bird is stuffed against its will.

Our village children enjoyed it all, so did the spectators. The girls invented their own dances, their own costumes. I thought the 'set-piece' poem was rather hard on my old friend Walter de la Mare: it rather tended to be mass-production of one particular poem. Why not a different little poem for each child? But it was a beginning; and a 'good effort'; and filled at least one spectator with hope for the future.

August 16, 1943

Harvest Story

A n artist settled in a corner of the field and with easel and old canvas before him (for he could not buy new) began to paint the happy scene of horses and tumbrils, the long lines of corn in shock, the clattering rusty horse-rake, the stack rising by the hedge, the pale blue sky and the distant sea with its white crinkle of waves on the sandy bar, the massed dark foliage of the sycamores and beeches of the carr by the river, the pale green meadows between wood and cornfield. He lit a big curved pipe and settled himself to an enjoyable afternoon in shadow, painting a grand English scene – 'Harvest in East Anglia.'

He watched one slow tumbril going laden to the stack, and another returning empty to the lines of shocks. He heard the shrill cry of the child leading the horse of the empty tumbril as it moved on down the line with slowly increasing burden – the warning cry of 'Hold ye!' The child's shrill Norfolk voice, product of clear, fine air and shrill east wind, was of the quality of the gull's cry as the bird seemingly elbowed whitely through the inverted blue of the sky. What could be more peaceful, more natural? He was a good artist, and when his completed picture hung eventually on the wall of some quiet London gallery, how it would bring simple truth to many an urban contemplator. Wars come and wars pass, but the corn grows and is harvested at the 'crown of the year.' Let others paint the surrealist effect of life beside the Lots Road Power Station, or the toad-like mottle of the bombers' wings overshadowing the tiny men loading bombs and belts of cannon-shells. That would pass, but this Old English scene would never pass. How fortunate was the farmer! What a serene mind he must have! Didn't know his good fortune! And so on, in enthusiastic vein, until the farmer, standing inarticulate, nearly believed him.

For the farmer saw another scene. He knew how slow and wasteful was the scene. There were too many intervals between the departure of an empty cart from the stack and the arrival of the next half-load.

He saw three men in khaki valiantly trying to pitch sheaves to two loaders on one tumbril! Five men to half-load one tumbril! The correct number should have been two; one man to pitch, one man on the load. But with the labour shortage, the farmer was only too glad for the soldiers' help; they were willing and did their best; but five men to one tumbril! Almost the farmer would have welcomed, not the lyrical artist, but the comic vision of a Heath Robinson, or that cartoonist who depicts naval scenes where everything goes wrong . . . one or two soldiers being pitched up with the sheaves, to disentangle themselves later as they progressed up the elevator. And that elevator!

It was a good elevator, but the power to turn its endless 'band' came from the only engine he could afford – a concrete mixer fitted with pulley. The concrete mixer weighed nearly a ton, and was a job to get into position. It had to be lugged and shoved just right, else its pulley fell off; and then it had to be lugged out again, and the cotter-pin sought among the stubble. To start it the belt had to be pulled by hand, and the flywheel weighed over a hundredweight. Whereas over the way a new red combine harvester was travelling round a rectangle of barley, cutting and threshing as it went. All done in one operation! True, a ribbon of straw was left behind on the stubble, probably to be burned (what a waste of humus), but in a few days that farmer would have finished his harvest, threshing and all. Our farmer dreaded threshing. It meant a stack trodden by numerous amateur boots, nobody to heave the 2-cwt sacks of grain into the tumbril until all was finished. Then it had to be shot in the barn, weighed and resacked, lifted again, and set on a lorry.

The artist didn't think much of that combine. The truly rural Old English scene was spoiled by it. It was too much like an urban idiom which the artist had come into the harvest field to escape. No tractors for him; only horses, tumbrils (preferably not on rubber tyres), and shrill cries of 'Hold ye.' Days, maybe weeks, after the combine over the boundary had done its work, this harvest would be going on. The artist knew nothing of that, as he puffed pleasantly his big curved pipe with the dropped bowl. 'Old England for ever,' he was chuckling. 'Life is short, art is long. I hope it never changes!' as he sploshed madder on the canvas. His picture, for £100 or more, would adorn the wall, perhaps, of some financier who had a lovely country place somewhere, where a model farm embellished the view, and all maintained on money legitimately gotten, perhaps from cheap foreign barley that had near-ruined North Norfolk before the war. Perhaps the art-patron would be a brewer, who wouldn't want a picture of a pre-war Polish or Hungarian harvest scene, where the corn was carried home even slower, by bullocks, and threshed out on a wooden barn floor all the winter months, by wooden flails fitted with universal joints made of cow-horn; and even so, could be bought at eight bob a sack at the port in England! No, he would want an English harvest scene, though he used foreign barley. And Hudson Gurney, peering out of Mr. Mottram's articles in the *E.D.P.* every Wednesday, would approve everything!*

The artist thought that all farmers grumbled; they were never satisfied. The farmer thought that the artist would learn something if he pitched with the long-handled fork for an hour or two. Or at threshing time, if he filled a hundred pulp-bags with 'flights', becoming gradually grey with dust in eye, nostril, hair, clothes and ear. Which was the truth, the sweating men and the endless sheaves, the cool perspective of the sedentary artist, or the small farmer who knew that his harvest costs would be about double what they should be? Easy money, painting a picture, he thought; but what did the farmer know of the early struggles of the artist, of the long hours of apprenticeship as a youth at a lithographer's bench, sixty hours a week for twelve shillings a week, in some dim underground basement of a backstreet? 'Will you put in five figures for one tumbril?' he inquired, 'two is the usual number.' 'Oh,' cried the artist, 'the number of figures doesn't matter. What I really want to get is the colours of the sea and sky before they change. What a lucky chap you are, to be living here all the year, in this marvellous Norfolk air. How would you like to be mewed up in a city most of your life?' Just then a horsefly bit him, and the long pipe dropped out of his mouth.

'Humph,' grunted the farmer, going away to the stack, for the elevator had stopped, and he knew that the pulley had come off the blanketty concrete mixer once more.

August 23, 1943

*R. H. Mottram, 1883–1971. Norfolk born and bred, he lived there all his life, and gave up his work as a bank clerk at the age of 44 to be a professional writer. He was the author of over sixty books, many of which were set in East Anglia, and is perhaps best known for *The Spanish Farm Trilogy, 1914–1918*, which was set in Flanders. *The Spanish Farm* was hailed as one of the most impressive novels of the Great War, and awarded the Hawthornden Prize in 1924.

Butterfly

An insect with tortoise-shell wings flitters at the window pane. Outside the sun shines and white clouds drift across the droning sky. Although I sit here in shadow, I know that over the hill-line, across the river at the bottom of the garden, and in the unseen folds of succeeding contours, the stubbles lie pale and bare. In some harvest fields lie lines of broken straw, where the combines have passed. Most of the corn has been gathered; and soon it will be the fifth year of the war.

Other butterflies drift over the garden. The cabbages are fretted by caterpillars. A marshman said he had seen hundreds of white butterflies coming in from the sea, from the direction of Holland. Three years and two months ago black smoke was drifting over the same sea from Holland. When a fine rain fell the tank and mudguards of the tractor and my coat and face and hands were streaked with smuts . . . the Rotterdam tanks were burning. Rumours came with the smoke, some of them as grimy, spread by human fear. Later the bombers came, and at night the sky flashed and the ground thudded. Today the incoming wings are of butterflies; tomorrow the cottage lights may be shining through the English dusk again.

After every major war people are tired. The reaction does not come at once. Those of us who remembered what happened last time know the theme of what might occur this time.

People were tired; most tired of all to do with the war. Nobody wanted to read a war-book. Publishers 'remaindered' their stocks; nobody bought them, even for a few pence. Thousands of ex-officers, recently demobilised, spent their 'blood-money', their gratuities, before looking round for a job. They dreaded the loss of the only world they knew, that of comradeship and excitement. Ex-scout pilots got jobs in civil aviation. Three of my friends bought an old plane and started an 'air-line' in Spain. It did not last beyond a few weeks. Back in England, one hired a barrel-organ and, wearing a mask, played in

the streets of London. Another started a poultry farm. It was bitter to lose the old feeling of comradeship. The world of youth seemed to perish at the Armistice. There was nothing to do. The comradeship was gone. As for the world before the war . . .

> Yet heaven looks smaller than the old dolls' home
> No nestling place is left in bluebell bloom,
> And the wide arms of trees have lost their scope.
> But the old happiness is unreturning:
> Boys' griefs are not so grievous as our yearning;
> Boys have no sadness sadder than our hope.

All the distinguished non-combatants published their memoirs. People who had not shared the fighting knew better secrets than those who had fought. Hundreds of thick books, priced between 18s. and 25s., arrived on the shelves of libraries. In the end these, too, were 'remaindered', and memoirs of tittle-tattle and gossip ceased. As for music, well, the public taste can be estimated from the sum of £30,000 reputed to have been made out of a song called 'Yes, we have no bananas.' Everyone in the streets and lanes sang or whistled it. The Corn Production Act was repealed, and farmers who had bought their farms at a high price found themselves facing ruin. Men were workless. In an effort to bring about the British Millenium, a General Strike was organised throughout England. Armoured cars protected food convoys from the London docks through the streets to Hyde Park, a vast food centre. Peers and bank clerks drove trains, trams and buses. Here and there in the larger and unhappier towns a motor car, taking people to work, was overturned by the mob. The strike ended. The first Socialist Government came to power only to find itself without power. The real power was in finance. Government was easier said than done.

It was now time for another kind of thought. The 'realistic' war-books appeared. One sold over 2,000,000 copies throughout the world. It debunked heroism; it described the charnel house and the despair of war. It included all that had been omitted from the battlefields; it screamed an aspect of truth. People said there can be no more war. War had been finally and completely debunked.

The slogans during the final year of 'Hang the Kaiser and bring to trial the war criminals' (which meant the losers) had long since died down. The Socialist Government, which was to have made a new world, fell. A few young members of Parliament set out to form a New Party. One by one they quit, leaving their leader in the wilderness, to rejoin the safer ranks of mediocrity. 'Realistic' war-books lost their interest; no one wanted to read them. The war was forgotten; reunion dinners of old comrades became thinner, and ceased altogether. Unemployment increased. Some men of thirty had never worked since leaving school; there was no work for them. Some children had never seen a plateful of cooked food; and when, after being evacuated in 1939 to a country cottage they were given a plate of roast beef and home-grown vegetables, they refused to eat such 'muck'. It had not come out of a tin.

The butterfly still flutters at the closed window. Ten feet away there is another window, wide open. Outside are the massed heads of hundreds of sunflowers. The butterfly is trying to get to the flowers through the glass. Its wings are frayed with vain beating.

The longing for the painted wings to escape into its vision of freedom is but part of the universal desire for a fuller life. Those who remember the film made from the 2,000,000-sale anti-war book, *All Quiet on the Western Front*, will recall how the soldier, at the end, was shot as his hand stretched out to touch a butterfly that had lit on the parapet. It was intended as a symbol of a sacrificed generation; innocent youth, desired beauty, having its life shattered. It was a sentimental and false symbolism because the butterfly was as innocent as the youth; and what virtue lies in the crushing of painted wings in a human hand? The film was overdone, like the book itself; the truth was not in it, even as the truth was not in the books published during the war. And all wars are essentially the same war.

The causes lie deep, but not so deep that one day clear-sight will not be able to make them plain. The time of clarity will come, even as the window will now be opened for the helpless fluttering wings to sail away in freedom.

August 30, 1943

A Farmer's Trials

The weather over the Straits of Dover has been such that half our barley had been lying in shock for some weeks. It was great fun for all of us – including the veterans – to pick up sodden sheaves and reset them, while the water turned us into maritime scarecrows. The original plan was to thresh off the shock, but the tackle could not come quite so early as that. One of our problems was the lack of anyone who could thatch; another was the stack-building, for we had no experienced stacker. Fifty-seven acres of barley and ten of wheat is about a day's work for modern industrialised farming with a team of self-propelled combine harvesters; but even with lorry, tractor-drawn tumbril and horse-drawn cart we found it impossible to get up even 10 acres a day. Nevertheless, our stack-builder, with only a season's experience of half a dozen stacks behind him, did better than I hoped. None of the stacks fell down; and only one bulged slightly. Clotted up, or covered with bitumen paper and net, they await the threshing tackle – and, we hope, calm weather over Dover and its environs.

Stack-building takes many years' experience to perfect. The other day, having to go a journey to buy some red-poll calves, I rejoiced to see, on the right of the road after passing the Woodrow Inn, a score or so of corn stacks which must be as good as any built and thatched in England. They are oval stacks of Lincolnshire pattern, I am told, and big, holding two hundred coombes, perhaps more. They were built better than many a jerry-house of the rent-purchase type; the visible butt-ends have been shaved symmetrically with a scythe. The straw at the eaves is straighter than many a cottage roof-ridge. I thought in passing that those stacks should be photographed and prints sent to *The Times* as an example of British farm-craft at its best. All the crops on that stretch of land, as I have seen during half a dozen years passing that way by car, are properly grown. On one of the fields in 1938 heaps of chalk were set out; today, after ewes folded on rye-grass and clover until late April, and the land plowed in May, and sugar-beet drilled afterwards, the small plants weeks behind other fields, that field has large and healthy beet, deep green in colour, while many of the others, a few miles on, are yellowing and starved-looking.

Harvesting on our farm hasn't always been like the oil-paintings this season. The artist with the big curved pipe got his idyllic picture in time. He didn't stop to help with the shocking. The hens have enjoyed the harvest better than anyone else. Put on the stubbles that were cleared and cultivated, they got in with a wild cockerel of the woods, who promptly led them to an easier life among the sheaves. Meanwhile, the hen-leader, an Italian cock, looking splendid with his bersaglieri feathers, had got tired, and was to be seen musing about alone, once in the company of a hen pheasant. The hens apparently welcomed the change of political regime. Regimentation in fold units appears to be 'out' for the time being. Freedom of range and nest-eggs tucked away in the wood is the fashion.

The democratic idea is spreading to other inhabitants of the farm. Freedom is in the air. The enslaved cats have left the barns and taken to the woods. There were eighteen of them, nearly all kittens, at one time, in the various buildings. They followed the children about and found rabbit nicer than black rat. The black rats are increasing on the farm. Where do they come from? The Old English decadent black rat, once near-exterminated by the Nordic grey rat, is coming back. Are they, too, affected by the ideological war among their two-legged superiors? Perhaps the County W.A.C. can tell us if they are on our side or not; for we do not, of course, wish to discourage any ally in the fight for civilisation. Is there a Free Rat Army somewhere?

Yesterday there were apples on the trees; today they are gone, and the owner did not pick them. Who did? Perhaps the Nordic rats have a scorched earth policy as they retreat. Or were the thieves of the species *Homo Rapiens*? Despite the artist with the curved pipe, our harassed thoughts turn to combine harvesting for next season. A small farm can afford only a small machine; can any reader give experience of the small model of the International or Allis-Chalmers harvester? We plan to plow up more old grass this autumn, and if the tide-flaps at the outfalls of the meadow-dykes (or rather the tidal intakes) are a success, the meadows, or some of them, hitherto water-slain for half the year, will go under the plow also. A combine seems to be the solution, provided one can arrange for timely drying of grain. All the combines of neighbouring farms seem to be the bigger models. Any information will be gratefully received.

For half an hour or so every night during the past week, before turning out the light, I have been reading a book called (ironically for us in the Straits of Dover) *No Rain in Those Clouds*, 'an account of John Smith's life and farming from 1862 to the present day' (Dent, 10s. 6d.). It's the real stuff, and a welcome change from so many farming books written by mere amateurs like myself. The country is Essex, near Chelmsford, and the author, John Smith's son, reminds me, in his style, of Richard Jefferies' early books, *The Amateur Poacher* and *Round About a Great Estate*.

At the bottom of the passage a door on the right led down some stone steps to the cellar. It was always beautifully cool, and kept the beer and butter in wonderful condition. In my grandfather's time there were two casks that held eight hogsheads and two casks that held five. When my father was young he was put inside the casks to lime-wash them before they were filled with beer. Before father was put in they tried the air with a candle; if the candle continued to burn brightly it was: 'All right, boy; in with you, and mind you scrape 'em well first!' Sometimes in winter when the pond rose from the rains, the cellar flooded suddenly, and people who went down without a light for a quick pint at supper-time got their feet wet.

A good little book, which will find a permanent place on my shelf. It is time that the real farmers began to write farming books; the refugees from the brain-gangs have had their say, and day. The only criticism I have to make of this book is, Why do the publishers impress on the last page the sentence 'COMPLIMENTARY COPY NOT FOR SALE'? With great respect I suggest to the publishers that metal perforating block should be sent forthwith to salvage.

September 6, 1943

The Corn is Threshed

Well, most of our corn is threshed and the straw stacks are covered with wire-netting against the equinoctial gales which we expect as usual towards the end of September. Equal night and equal day; twelve hours' light, twelve hours' darkness; and the balance gradually dropping to darkness once again. Has there been a spring? Has anyone seen the summer? I caught a glimpse of the summer, one Sunday on the marshes, when the tide was flowing even and sky-blue-smooth, when the children and I got on our bicycles and forgot (or I did) the war and the farm. I saw the summer again in other glimpses, when passing the hard tennis court in the grounds of the Old Hall, and seeing someone in white flannels snicking a tennis ball over the net. Owing to the generosity of the new owner of this historic house (a pig, crest of the old family, is to be seen still on one of the keystones of an outbuilding) the village has been able to form a tennis club and take turns on the new court (1938) with soldiers and airmen free for a few hours from their duties.

I wondered what Squire 'Turnip',* once the owner of all this land and seashore and farms and buildings, would have said to a sight of a farm labourer, after his 9-hour day, enjoying himself with a racquet. Was caoutchouc (rubber) used in his time? Or did they play only

---

*Charles, Lord Townshend (1674–1738) was a diplomat turned farmer. 'Turnip' Townshend, as he was called in his later years, had a long and distinguished career in politics, playing a vital part in negotiating both the Union with Scotland (1707) and the Treaty of Utrecht (1713). After a quarrel with Walpole in 1730 he retired from political life to concentrate on farming his estates in Norfolk. He improved the quality of the soil, much of which was a sandy swamp, by draining it and adding manure and marl. He popularised the idea of growing roots and artificial grasses between corn crops, and this Norfolk four-course rotation of turnips, barley or oats, clover and wheat made the production of cattle fodder an important part of arable farming. This enabled farmers to feed their livestock through the winter instead of slaughtering it in the autumn; fresh meat could therefore be eaten all the year round, instead of salted meat in the winter months.

squash racquets with leather balls stuffed with feathers? Times change; the great landlords depart; speculators buy and resell to lovers of old beams and crumbling brickwork, who spend much money on restoration and then die; the modernised interiors echo to the noises of schools or country clubs (if in 'good' districts), and nowadays as barracks, hostels for evacuees, and headquarters for bombed-out business executives. Today village girls of fourteen paint their lips and wear their finger-nails long like Chinese Mandarins, via, of course, the film heroines of Hollywood. At three o'clock the farm labourer is black with dust and grime of threshing; at seven o'clock he is in 'immaculate white flannels', and neatly flicking a tennis ball over the net; while the family ghost, long since laid by wireless, daily newspapers, water-repelling cement and prontosil, simply doesn't know what it is all about.

Personally, I am glad to see such things as tennis coming to the villages, and sports clubs, and maybe (who knows?) one or two of those new cottages we have read so much about. Our village club is self-supporting. That is as it should be; every tree must grow and stand by its own roots. I remember the old squire of a Devon village some years ago, just after the last war, trying to start a football club. He lent the ground; he gave and erected the goalposts; someone presented the football and flags for the linesmen; he built a little place where coats, etc., could be hung, and a few people sit and watch in cold weather. He wasn't a rich man; indeed, his place was mortgaged, and within twenty years he was sold up and went to live in a little house in a town. But while he could he tried to help things; but would the village get up a football team? The village would not; and they grumbled because the old fellow had not provided them with shorts, boots, stockings and jerseys. His efforts caused only grievances. That was a year before the General Strike of 1926.

I fancy that would not have happened in East Anglia, for, generally speaking, the people here are, in my limited observation, more self-reliant and independent. Their blue eyes and long heads reveal a racial type other than that of the round-headed, brown-eyed Celts of the West Country. One of the first things that struck me as a foreigner, coming from the West, was the comparative honesty of the East Anglian villager. The complete absence of slyness was remarkable. Not so amiable; but more upright. East Anglia is, again generally speaking, peopled by the Nordic type; it's a commonplace to speak of the Danish, Icelandic, Scandinavian, Flemish, Viking percolations of the early centuries. It's ... but what about the harvest and the threshing? I didn't sit down to write all this. The white flannel reference to summer was meant only in passing. Back to the dusty faces around the threshing box.

We got ten coomb an acre, of good yellow, mellow barley. The rains did that, as the corn stood in shock, days, weeks after the combine over the hedge had gone and only blackened ribbons of burnt straw showed where it had passed (and incidentally, what grains were dropped on the ground). Drying winds and sun followed the rains, and when the drum came we had organised local help from other small farmers, who lent us their men; we lend them ours in return, and thus the dread of threshing short-handed is removed. It's what is wanted in the village; people getting more together. 'One's neighbour is oneself'; how true is that principle of living!

The hot drying winds made me anxious of fire; but fortunately the majority of farm-workers know better than to smoke around the stack. I saw only one man smoking out of ten men working; and was grateful for the good manners of the nine. For to smoke at the stack is to be guilty of bad manners.

I mentioned the hankering some of us have for a combine harvester, and asked for advice; and hereby give thanks to one or two people who have generously replied. The best scheme I've read was from a farmer near Diss who lets 2000 head of poultry range over the stubbles, thus feeding themselves on the dropped grains and also spreading the straw and manuring the land. Another correspondent was not so constructively helpful; he demanded to know what was wrong with horses and the good old-fashioned reaper? Nothing is wrong with them; both are well maintained on our farm. So is the good old-fashioned scythe, and we also have a reaping hook and a flail. Also, we have a good old-fashioned wooden 'firkin', or 'bottle', and sometimes it is filled with good old-fashioned cider. Even as I finish this article I see an old-fashioned pink china pot coming my way, and soon the spigot will be out, the tap turned, and with a bit of bread and cheese (which must be eaten with sharp old cider) it will be washing some of the chaff and calder down this throat.

September 13, 1943

Journey to the West

It is always with a feeling of settled satisfaction that I sit in a carriage of the 8 a.m. train from the station, heading for London. Inevitably it is a rush to get there on time, and the usual margin is three minutes. Bag on rack, book in pocket, packet of toast-and-bacon sandwiches on the seat beside me. Harvest is over, most of the corn threshed, sold and loaded away; now there is nothing to think of but the tiled roofs moving past as the train rounds a curve and the little coastal town is left behind.

At first the journey is an adventure. One is alone in the carriage, looking out over the marshes, some in stubble after corn has been carted, but most of them still in grass and thistle. Cattle graze on them or lie chewing the cud among the irregular rows of rusty iron cake-pans. No cake – linseed, cotton, crushed sunflower seed – in them nowadays; and yet the beasts seem just as big as before. A record harvest, the newspapers say, and gotten up in record time. My time of anxiety, of sodden shocks, is over. As the wheels trundle over the expansion-breaks in the rails the feeling of satisfaction remains, and I open the packet of sandwiches. If I don't eat them now, before the junction, I'll miss the chance of solitary mastication. It is much nicer to eat alone.

After the junction, with its change into the London train, life becomes less simple. There are many people. The carriage is soon filled. Someone makes the inevitable joke – 'Is your journey really necessary?' That someone, if he had a dog, would probably call it Monty. That dog's father, if in the same possession, would have been called Bonzo; and its grandfather, Rover.

A dash past the barrier at the town, to get a newspaper, and to read that perhaps the war will not be over next week, or at Christmas, after all. Italy to be a battlefield after all; and the carriage, too, it seems, though a polite and stoical one. Corridors full, and three standing by our legs. The train lurches off, and a fat young woman with a lieutenant's badge of rank collapses with startled apologies into my lap. I offer her the last of the sandwiches, which she declines graciously as I give up my seat and depart for the guard's van, to find it packed with recumbent figures in khaki. After a further search I find a seat in a third class carriage, and sit down discreetly in it, wondering if I shall be liable for the difference in cost of tickets. Maybe; everything is topsy-turvy in war-time.

So to the South, from the green and thistly pastures to the areas of bricks and mortar, and into the darkness of the terminal station. Outside it isn't so bad; the spaces made by the clearances of bombed buildings are pleasant, sun and air replace dinginess and shadow. Indeed, the journey to the centre of the town is nowadays quite pleasant; the smarting of the country-eye is no more, gone with the slight carbon-monoxide headache of peace-time. Will they build again in these wide and pleasant areas, purified by fire, where water gleams and wild duck paddle, and the rose-bay willow-herb loosens its parachute-seeds on the moving airs? Let us have grass and water and trees and flowers – let us be unbusiness-like about it. It will pay in the end.

So to London, and the uniforms everywhere, of many nationalities, just as in the last war – but not quite the same. The uniforms this time are of khaki, and the basic pattern is British, for the Europeans and those of the Empire. Basic uniforms – basic English – the language of diplomacy of the future. The pound and the dollar are amalgamated, and the basic power of the union is gold. Trade shall be free among the nations, and the talisman of freedom shall be gold; there's the basic war-aim in a sentence of basic English. And as I scribble this in the bar of a little inn of the West Country, within hearing of the waves pounding the rocky shores of the Eastern Atlantic, while the Devon burring speech mingles with the transatlantic dialect of the United States, I remember the story of the farmers and tradesmen and preachers leaving this very coast a little while ago in a ship called the *Mayflower*, seeking new lands in the New World, because England was too small. There was a colony founded there, wasn't there, and a little trouble about something or other? Well, it looks as though the trouble was over; and I don't think I'm giving away any secrets by stating that the *Mayflower* appears to have made a return voyage, and all because England seemed in danger of growing even smaller. The farmers and tradesmen and preachers, or their kith and kin, are back again, drinking the scrumpy cider again and the beer, and generally, by their behaviour (and I can only speak as I find) being a credit to the old country. Basic English? Well, England, as you know, is a mixture of all sorts of races, so perhaps with truth we can say, Yes, basic English. Let it be so, in big things and in little things, in the villages and in the towns – let there be sun and air and light – let these rule, rather than dollar or pound or mark or franc or rouble – let there be basic gold, but not for its own sake or profit at any price. It's time the world had a break. Someone with upturned chevrons on his tunic sleeve – a top-sergeant, I think – is holding out another pint of scrumpy, and so if you'll allow me . . .

September 22, 1943

Love's Labour Lost

My watch had stopped. It might have been the rain. For five days the rain had fallen on the fields and beaten on the leaves of the hill-top beeches. All day I had sat in the hut, by a fire of oak logs, wondering what to do until 8 o'clock, when I supposed I would walk down the mile-long hill and enter the pub known as the Lower House, and there stand among three-score other people in the little bar and be talked to. This was my holiday in glorious Devon, and for all of the days it had been raining. Sheaves of wheat and oats stood in the sodden fields – at least, once they had been sheaves of corn, now they were sodden bundles of rotten straw, and the corn had been growing so long that even the idea of turning bullocks out among the shocks was no good. The green blades of the wheat were over six inches in length.

My watch had stopped. It hung on the rusty nail driven into the brick chimney breast of the open hearth. The hut had been empty for most of the year, and mildew was on the oak boards of the floor. A mouse had been gnawing one of the boards, which years ago had been 'fed' with linseed oil. They were old boards, hand sawn several centuries ago, and had come out of a derelict mansion near Eggesford, above the River Taw. The mildew grew out of the linseed.

That mouse must have had a partiality, as they say, for linseed. He was an industrious little fellow, too, for in the corner of the hut, when last I had been there, a lump of putty had been resting. There had been quite two pounds of putty in that lump. Day after day, and maybe night after night, that mouse had squatted by the putty and eaten of it. Week after week the rodent had returned to its solitary feast, until all was consumed. No, to be precise, all was not consumed, for the lump of putty had been converted into thousands, into tens of thousands, of little elongated pilules only a few inches away from its original massive position. What the mouse got out of his hours of mastication I do not know, but I have an idea that the work

76

did not pay for itself. Consider the labour cost of mastication, swallowing, digestion, and all the other processes involved in turning a mouthful of putty into a pilule of putty! He got the oil, I suppose, but it could not have paid him, as farmers say. Well, it was his business. My putty was still there: a little oil added to it, and it would be as good as ever.

My watch had stopped. What was the time? Did the time matter? Wasn't I on holiday? It was, perhaps, judging by the greyness of the day, about 9 a.m. I had nothing to do until 9 p.m., when I supposed I would walk down to the old pub, drink cider or beer I didn't want, hear the same old stories about Dunkirk by the man who wasn't (they said) ever there, and then walk a mile uphill again in rain or starlight, from 200 feet above sea level to 900 feet, enter the hut, undress, climb up to the shelf, called the bedroom, or Doves' Hotel, as some visitor had chalked on a candle-blackened beam, and then try and sleep, while just by my head, beyond the plaster of the coving ceiling the *ric-ric-rac* of a gnawing mouse would continue, despite shouts, thumps, bangs, curses and other propaganda, most of the hours of darkness. O most industrious mouse, I would muse, thou hast converted my putty from lump to pilules innumerable, and now thou are engaged in eating my roof! But when the effects of the scrumpy cider had worn off, the bangs and thumps and curses would succeed the homily.

My watch had stopped. Heavens, it was Friday, and possibly 9 a.m. or later. I had not yet washed, shaved, had breakfast, or written my article for the *E.D.P.* The London train left the village, four miles distant, at 10.50 a.m. I had no transport; even my old raincoat, left hanging in the hut, was tattered and in holes (that mouse again, or his co-racials, plus a veritable *Luftwaffe* of moths). But my copy must leave by that train.

Hearing shouts in a neighbouring field (smallholder and dog trying to round up sheep to 'fly' them), I went out and asked the time. A quarter past nine. So things must move swiftly. In an hour I had shaved, washed, fed and written the article; borrowed a bicycle from an astonished woman admiring the view from the hilltop, jumped on and flown down the hill, learning as the speed approached wind-whistling in the cavities of the ears, the brakes were brakes only nominally. And half the army seemed to be present, in jeeps, peeps and other vehicles. Somehow we did not collide, but managed to reach the station as the train was steaming there, make contact with the guard, and for a fee of 4d. assure that the article was posted in London that night, to reach London Street in Norwich by Saturday – in time for Press on the Sunday. I congratulated myself on my making it, only to learn later that it didn't arrive on Saturday after all, but on the following Monday. However, like the mouse with the putty, I enjoyed the incident.

September 27, 1943

The God Gold

The other night I went with the chairman of the local branch of the Young Farmers' Club to the second meeting of that branch. It was a district made famous by one of the outstanding names in British farming history. Here began that tract of country where several square miles of rich grazing land, some of it now growing corn, had been reclaimed from the sea; where in the past hundreds of thousands of trees had been planted in a sandy, windswept waste, a great house built and a wall put around the miles of deer park and a pheasant covert, and light land which of olden time grew only poor scanty grass was made to grow wheat, after deep pits had been dug, and the marl spread on the thin soil. The rent-roll consequent on all this work had been increased 1000 per cent; which meant prosperity for hundreds of families, an assured livelihood, and a healthy social life; for that life was based on honest hard work and service.

Mindful of the tradition of the countryside, I wondered what I should see of agricultural keenness among the Young Farmers of the new-formed club.

Historians will search the files of local papers for authentic details of our times. They will not find many. Even the weather will not be mentioned. Imagination reveals the archaeologists of the future, peering diffidently, scientifically, among ruins, probing heaps and finding with fast-beating hearts some local fragments of china, and perhaps (tremendous excitement!) a genuine, yes we think it is genuine, a genuine fragment of very rare early rubber, that quaint stuff made from the sap of a tree, one of the kind which grew in the extinct civilisation of Ancient Malaya, where the anciently-called hotels and clubs of the white men alone reveal, by their accumulations of broken bottles, a glimpse into the past.

It will be for the historians of the future to tell of this our age. Let us join them for a moment. There are two characteristic signs of an extinct civilisation in all this district. One, the curious hollows in the fields; it is thought that once upon a time the natives cared for their land, for husbandry, that they actually dug up the thicker sub-soil in order to mix it with the upper sand, in order to grow wheat, that staple diet of the people in those days. Later, the wheat berry was de-vitalised, all its goodness taken away, in the interests of what was called Big Business. It was the age of the god of gold; and one of the unwritten rules of this religion was that a man had generally to conceal his paramount desire to worship the god. But the religious feeling was most strong; and in the end such things as marling the land became uneconomic, or 'not done', to use a phrase of the times; and farming became a 'mug's game'. (Professor Parwitt states that the term 'mug's game' was derived from the 'mug' which used to hold beer; the inference being that farmers 'going downhill', used to seek consolation in tilting more and more mugs of beer, and even more potent drink.)

The modern archaeological theory is that the vast grass-grown tracts, which occur in practically every flat area in the district, followed inevitably on the worship of the god gold; that the disuse of the marlpits was only a sign of the neglect of husbandry and the disintegration of family and village life. That the prolonged tracts occur in most of the flat areas of the old Europe is thought to indicate that the phenomenon was not confined to Britain, let alone the region under the survey of our Field Expedition today.

There were attempts, we may be sure, to continue the opening up of the marlpits, rather than the laying down of the mysterious tracts. Dr Krarkle, whose invention with the use of the Z ray brought back vibrations of the past (until it blew up with the shattering of the atom), always declared that he could see the tracts being made in his Radioscope, and hear the very words of those engaged in the mysterious work. But the doctor's invention perished with him; and perhaps we shall never know the truth of his contention, or rather theory. He had set himself to prove that the god gold eventually turned mankind insane, reversing all their virtues and skill in natural living and turning them into individuals who cared nothing for the job, but only for the profit they could get in the easiest way. Thus cheap foreign food came to the island as tribute to the god gold, and both farmers and the land suffered. Life, like the soil in many places, became acid.

Dr Krarkle claims that he heard on his Radioscope an actual voice telling another that he made over a hundred quid a week, and not having a banking account, there was no record of it, and he wouldn't have to pay any tax, income or E.P.T. Many times, the old doctor used to emphasise, the words E.P.T. were caught on his Radioscope, as well as a most extraordinary confusion of lies on the air of that period. Indeed, just before the old scientist vanished in a cloud of radio-dust, when the atom exploded for the only recorded time in history, he claimed to have solved the problem of the phases before the final disintegration of the entire species of *Homo Rapiens*. The whole aim was for gold; but it was, after all, only paper; and the more paper there was the slower but longer and wider grew the tracts covering the fertile surface of the land, and the less there was to buy in the shops. The children on leaving school got the same idea as their elders; despite a few poor films advertising the joys of watching a pig with a straw in your mouth, of thatching, shearing sheep, milking a cow (taking turns with twenty others to do this, and not a pail kicked over), no one thought of the land. It was the hardest work and the least rewarded, judging solely by the standards of the god of gold, or, rather, paper. On religious grounds whole cities were wiped out, and millions perished, until at last all the beer-barrels stood empty, for there was nowhere to grow barley, and no one to get it in anyway. Only then, when the beer stopped, did the tracts crossing all the fertile areas cease to be built. There was nothing left to eat or drink: only the paper.*

Which is perhaps not unconnected with my visit the other night to the local branch of the Young Farmers' Club, where, beside the chairman and his vice-chairman, two small boys and a Land Girl, I found myself one of six adults sitting dolefully around in a frustrated circle because there was nothing to do. Unfortunately, Dr Krarkle's invention is not available, and so we shall have to wait for more enlightened times for the full story of Cause and Effect.

October 4, 1943

---

*Over eighty airfields were built in East Anglia during the war. In 1942 an urgent airfield building programme was accelerated, in readiness for the arrival of the US 8th Air Force. The individual cost of a single bomber airfield at this time was £990,000.

The Magpie's Nest

L ying here on the western headland, with the great waves of the Atlantic, driven by the gale, breaking on the reef below, I recall soldiers at rest after battle looking at a daily newspaper and reading an account of that battle, and of the company commander throwing down the paper in contempt. It was after the retreat on the Somme, when the Germans had withdrawn to their *Siegfried Stellung*. On that occasion the direct cause of rage was the mention of skylarks singing through the barrage that fell upon Monchy le Preux, Fontaine Croiselles, and Bullecourt, in the abortive attack in which he had lost many of his men. That company commander had been in the battle, which stopped before the massive entanglements of the *Siegfried Stellung*, or Hindenburg Line; he had heard many noises, but none of them from the throat of a skylark.

Yet the war correspondent's account was not untrue. The man wrote what he saw and heard. I did not 'go over' in that particular assault, and so I watched the barrage comfortably from a wheatfield a couple of miles back. It was timed for dawn; zero hour was at 4.20 hours. About 4.19 hours, in the hush of darkness just beginning to give way to a spectral pallor in which I could see the wire of our reserve line a few yards away as a blackish mass, I heard a lark break into song above me. It was followed by another, and then by a third; and I waited, with the stillness of expectation, while the singing grew faint and shrill, as the birds flew up towards the paling stars. There was a great ragged orange flash, oval and instant, from the four 9.2 howitzers in the chalk quarry on my right. And while the flash went through my eyes into my mind the sky became one great raging sea of light. Hundreds of batteries were firing. The 18-pounders were far in front, in the open valley; 60-pounder counter-battery guns stabbed whitely beyond the sunken road, merging into the orange belch of howitzers – 6-inch, 9.2, and 12-inch behind me in the next valley. Thousands of great fingers of light were flickering to the zenith, while

the earth shook and rumbled with one continuous drumming reverberation. And through the intense exhilaration of this massive light and sound, while red, green and golden rockets arose from the distant Hindenburg Line, to break above the reef of fire where shells were bursting, I heard, faint and high and thin, like the jingling of the tiniest silver chain, the song of the skylark.

A few hours later I met one of our company limping back, with a shrapnel ball through his left calf. He was cheerful and happy, with thoughts of Blighty uppermost in his mind. He told me of a magpie he had seen flying into a low thorn bush on the downs, just before he had been hit. 'One for sorrow they say, sir, but I reckon it's one for luck, as far as No. 1 is concerned.' The attack had failed so completely that no reinforcements were to go up, so I thought I would walk through Croiselles, a broken village, and see how things were. That is the excuse I gave myself; but my real motive was to find the magpie's nest, and so to get an egg, with luck, for my collection at home. For the war had broken into my consciousness only in that spring, and summer now had no meaning. Before the war I had lived only to be in the woods and fields, with the birds.

Only a little stuff was falling among the ruins of the village, sending up the usual fountains of smoke and brick dust. I passed a line of troops with Vickers and Lewis guns under the railway embankment, and so came to the open country beyond. I remember pausing before a dump of tins and other stuff, including a heap of egg-shaped coal-dust brickettes, where several German helmets were thrown about. Among them were Bavarian shakos, and the old 1914 *Picklehaube*.

83

Did I want one? To send home as a souvenir? But of what? No, the magpie's possible nest was more important. I had dreamed for years of getting a magpie's egg.

I walked on up the gradual slope, sometimes pausing to watch a salvo of howitzer shells falling on the skyline like Atlantic breakers on a reef on a loppy day. A few dead lay here and there, in the curiously immobile attitudes of men killed by machine-gun fire.

A few small thorns were visible a couple of hundred yards ahead. As I pondered the expressions on the faces of the dead, I wondered if it would be safe to go so far forward. It was curiously quiet, except for the whizzbangs and 4.2's searching for the field batteries in Croiselles; and for the hollow reports behind me followed by the corkscrewing swishing of howitzer shells in the blue overhead. Dare I go forward to those thorns? Surely they were not more than 300 yards from the crest of the slope, just over which lay the first trench of the Hindenburg system. How about snipers in pits in front? Well, I could always drop into a shell hole.

It was a fine spring day, and yet I could not feel myself to be part of it. My feeling was entirely impersonal; this was not the English spring, and therefore it meant nothing to me. My real life was as remote from me as the dead lying so still on the torn grass. (It was after the war that one got the full reaction; and if the soldiers had made the peace, instead of the politicians who kept the home fires burning, it might not have become an alien world once more.)

I got to the thorn trees without mishap, though my heart beat fast as I approached. Sure enough, there was a magpie's nest in one of them, and only about six feet from the ground. It was just as I had read in books: a dome of thorns on top, to keep away other corvine robbers! While I was gingerly putting my hand through the spines to the hollow nest below, a Yorkshire voice said that it were 'too 'igh for 'im to get at th' eggs, else he'd 'v sooked 'em already.' Turning, I saw a cheerful ruddy face grinning at me from the ground a few yards away. He was leaning back in a slight hollow, with several water bottles and bayonet-stabbed tins of bully beef around him. He told me that he was one of a patrol which had set out, many nights before, to report on the enemy wire. The patrol had been surprised and dispersed by hand grenade and machine-gun fire. His left arm had been smashed, and he had lain down all the next day, crawling at night to the cover of the thorn trees. There he had stopped, 'knowing the boys would be back,' maintaining life on iron rations and water taken from the dead.

His arm was off below the elbow, and maggots were around the stump. These, he declared, had kept the wound 'from getting too proud.' Had I a fag? Then, seeing I was an officer, he said he was sorry. Fortunately I had some cigarettes, and we smoked and rested and talked, while the long afternoon turned to twilight, when I helped him (for he was very weak) back to the line of outposts, which were outside the ruins of the village. Half-way back we both remembered that we had forgotten to find out if there were any eggs in the nest. We said goodbye at the first-aid post, and I left him quite cheerful, thinking of going home, and making jokes about his arm. I always remember that day as one of the best in my life.

War is not all pure evil; there are moments when one lives beyond the 'little ego', in what is called comradeship, a quality of living which is scarcely to be written. It was the loss of this quality in post-war life which made the 'peace' so empty.

October 11, 1943

Little Summer: A Pause

The other day I walked up the hill towards a neighbouring farm, where I was a guest for the shooting. It was one of those calm, sunny days of early October when the spirit of the English country-side is seen at its best – in tranquillity. The blaze of summer was gone, the rush of the spring was forgotten; it was now autumn, and for a space the earth could rest. Nothing was growing, nothing was visibly perishing. The trees stood still. Not a leaf was falling, except for the touch of a wood pigeon's wing as it wheeled out of the distant wood. The cycle of birth, growth and decay stood, for the moment, still.

Over all the fields and plantations seen from the crest of the hill a faint haze was hanging. The land sloped away gently until woods and hedges and corn stacks were dissolved in golden haze. Far away a tractor crawled across a field of stubble, and farther still a team of horses was setting in, so small as to show no movement. The air was dry; gossamers were spreading across hedge and stubble, the spiders making their last journeys before hibernation.

A man with a mind preoccupied by other things cannot enjoy 'nature'. 'Nature', indeed, is but a mood of man. It has no existence apart from that mood. Beauty is perceived only by a mind void of other mental pictures, or fragmentary thoughts. If a man is worried he cannot merge thoughtlessly into a landscape and feel its beauty. For a man has these feelings within himself; they do not come altogether from without.

To take an extreme case, that of a soldier advancing into the wonderful scenery around Naples. ('See Naples and die,' some artist once said, meaning that to see such natural beauty was the climax of life.) That man, under intense mortar and bomb fire, sees nothing of the beauty. His thoughts are quickened by fear and anxiety; the landscape means nothing at all to him.

Only a man free of worry would have seen what my idle self saw on that morning. I felt a happiness to be in such surroundings; but most

86

of that happiness, the harmony of colour of tiled roofs and yellow stacks and darkness of trees was due wholly to the fact that the new Essex gilt had pigged nicely, that the bullocks were off the wet meadows and safely on the grassy hills, the turkeys liked their new home and were fine young birds, the ducks were laying, the farm was supporting me and not I the farm, and at last I had shot the wild cockerel which had lured all the hens away to the woods. The shabby paint of the bathroom was now hidden under a new coat, after four years of impotent saying to myself, 'I really must do this' – and leaving it at that. I felt good because the visit of the District Claims Officer, in the matters of a shot heifer, broken gates and smashed flint, had been pleasant, the matters suitably and swiftly settled. And not least, I was for once not late for an engagement; indeed, I was well on time.

For several minutes I leaned over a gate and forgot the war, the big world war and my little personal war. Free of material details in the mind, I could share the life of 'nature' about me – the spider hanging on the gatepost, the bird on the hedge, the lone gull gliding across the sky. Life was good, and England, as revealed by the landscape, was the best place to be in. And the farming life, well, in spite of its difficulties – which ultimately meant the difficulties of my own nature – it was the only life for me. I thought with satisfaction of what Bob, the travelling engineer with the threshing drum, had said a few weeks previously, 'You've done well on this farm. We've threshed your corn every year, and it gets better each season.' Authentic praise from one who had spent most of his life with that 'tackle', as his father had before him!

Usually a poor shot, in an hour or so I found that my first five shots brought down four partridges and a hare. I noticed with satisfaction (or self-assurance) that the more brilliant guns on my left and right were not always hitting their birds. It was the start of the season, of course; perhaps they were in a mental muddle?

For I used to think, in my solitary goings and comings, that I alone was one to get into a muddle, that I was the only farmer who couldn't cope, usually making mistakes and unable to deal with matters that real farmers took in their stride; until a deeper acquaintanceship with others told me that the farm where things always went easily and according to plan probably did not exist in peace-time, and certainly not in war-time. With what consolation did I once hear from a big and successful agriculturist these words, 'I just don't go near the farm nowadays. If I do, it only causes trouble. So I keep away and let them get on with it.'

War is destructive, and not all the harm is material. All of us lose so much of our daily vitality owing to the war. War is frustration of most of the human virtues, though not of all the human qualities. Whether we know it consciously or not, war saps much of our vital hope and energies. I put it at 40 per cent loss for most sensitive people. Even those with simple jobs, who have the least nervous wastage, are affected by the strain of the times. Their subconscious thoughts are not happy or truly free. Thus, in mental reaction, we hope for a better world 'after the war'. Such longings are the measure of our discontent.

Food, too, has much to do with one's thoughts. A well-fed man sees not the same world as a man who lacks sufficient energy-making 'grub'. The rations of farm workers are poor and inadequate for the heavy daily work. No man can knock beet all day on a bit of bread and margarine, flavoured by a scrape of jam, with a piece of cheese and a couple of cold potatoes, washed down by a bottle of cold tea. Beauty is in the eye of the beholder; but its foundations are in a good square meal.

October 18, 1943

Pheasants and Partridges

It will be interesting to see what *Picture Post* makes of a shoot that took place in our district last week. My shooting goes in with my neighbour's; we are partners, he the senior, I the junior, of the shooting over the two farms.

In war-time farmers are allowed petrol to get to their friends' places for the purpose of shooting. What, I hear an urban critic murmuring, petrol in war-time for *shooting*? Yes, sir, for shooting. There were nine of us last week, including Mr Macdonald Hastings, of *Picture Post*, and those nine guns accounted for over one hundred brace of partridges and about one hundred and seventy pheasants. Reckoned on economic grounds alone, five gallons of petrol bringing the 'guns' to the rendezvous and taking them back again, produces a dinner for about one thousand people (food-hogs excluded).

The word *pheasant* produces sometimes a curious reaction among some people. I belong to a Bohemian club in London, where one sees the faces of such celebrities as A.G. Street, George Graves, Basil Cameron, Charlie Clapham, Gillie Potter, Mark Hambourg, Benno Mosievitch, James Agate, to name several of hundreds encountered at random in the dining-room. Knowing that food was likely to be scarce, I had an idea early in 1941 of sending the game we did not want at home to the club. Asked the invariable, 'How's the farm?' (although I notice no one ever says to Mark Hambourg, 'How's the piano?') I replied what was then uppermost in my mind: the fact that so many soldiers had been searching for wild pheasants' nests in the hedges and along the verges of woods that I feared there would not be many birds in the coming season.

'Does that matter very much?' demanded my interlocutor, with sideway narrowing eyes. I felt myself to be suitably reproached; half the club premises were still smoking from one of the biggest blitzes on London. Rome burned while Nero fiddled; Drake might continue his game of bowls while the Spanish Armada was approaching; but it was too much, with the bar of the Barbarian Club blasted away and most of the bedrooms blitzed, that all one of the eccentric members found to remark was that his pheasants' eggs had been pilfered. 'We deserve to lose the war,' my questioner muttered as he swallowed another large whiskey-and-soda.

The facts of fishing, shooting, hunting and other field sports are not generally appreciated by the urban critics of these so-called pastimes. Let us take a detail that would shock a hyper-sensitive humanitarian eating a nut steak at a food reform centre. I saw a sportsman hit, but not kill, a partridge. He picked it up and cracked its head with his teeth. What barbarianism! exclaims our pale, sandal'd food-reformer, as he crunches what might have been a beautiful living tree in his jaws. Once I told a woman, in the act of drowning kittens in a pail, that it was kinder to bury them alive. She was horrified. Yet to bury new-born kittens alive is short and merciful compared with the slow and prolonged misery of drowning them. (In case any gentle humanitarian wants to shoot me for stating this, let me hasten to add that our farm-house has given shelter to many a half-drowned kitten rescued by the small boys of the family from the nearby river.) The partridge-biter was in truth a nice, gentle creature, invariably kind to children and considerate towards other men; whereas the shuddering nut-cracker was an anti-blood sports crusader, and through laceration of thin nerve-coverings, an invariable trouble-maker in the home. I speak as a mere observer of the human scene, and not as a critic. (One of the most sensitive and idealistic men alive today has, through frustration of his *finer* feelings, been one of the main causes of this present war. And in this connexion one would like to postulate that the man who bites a game-bird's head, to kill it swiftly, is much too phlegmatic to be a disturber of men's souls, and therefore, eventually, of their peace.)

These random thoughts came to me as I rode, with a score or more of guns and beaters, with their dogs and daughters and all their *impedimenta* (let us freedom-loving scribes use all the hybrid words we may, before Basic English rations our phrases) along a sandy drift or lane, huddled on a great platform on wheels drawn by a chuffing tractor. Who is that young man, hatless and wild-haired, an Irish look about his eyes, fixing his Leica to his socket, adjusting swiftly the lens, then clicking the shutter? He is no other than Mr Mac Coombs, who, with Mr Macdonald Hastings, has come to get the 'low-down' on our inarticulate selves.

Let us get the low-down on them first. They are everywhere, peering and listening. Nothing is missed. At luncheon a gun raises a bottle of beer (made of Norfolk barley, since the Polish variety is temporarily unavailable for the financial overlords) and instantly Mr Mac Coombs has got him. A dog yawns; tongue, teeth, gullet, flews, all are snapped. Observe the well-known figure of one of England's leading Black Pig breeders down there by the Common; he raises his gun a score of times in a minute, forty times in two minutes, sixty times in three minutes, and not a bird in sight! And always the peering figure, Leica to eye, hovering, darting low, weaving like a mongoose, then striking . . . *click.* Another one, *click.* Our Black Pig expert is being groomed for stardom, no doubt.

It was an enjoyable day, and not least because of the presence of the two Macs in our cottage afterwards, where we drank some matured old perry and a bottle of Algerian wine which had been mouldering for a score or so of years in a box, with a few others, brought up from Devon. Dog does not eat dog and journalist does not trespass on the territory of journalist; but as they are going to reveal us in their *Picture Post* we thought we would get in our little revelation first. Yet supposing pictures and 'story' do not appear, but instead something more urbanly utilitarian (ugh, this base English has got us), such as How Socks are Knitted for Sailors or Gas from Coal (and ninety-nine uses of Tar), then we shall have been properly sucked in (to use basic Norfolk).

October 25, 1943

Plowman's Folly

When Stephenson invented the 'Rocket'; when Louis Pasteur proved that anthrax was a germ in sheep which killed them; when the motor car was invented; when the Wright Brothers flew in a heavier-than-air machine; when wireless became a popular possibility and the gramophone interests opposed it as likely to ruin their business; when ... but one could go on indefinitely. All these and other new ideas were greeted as ridiculous, impracticable, ruinous, etc. Why, even in my small sphere, I've been told that mites are 'nature' to horses (therefore it's no good trying to 'get rid of 'em'), that cows make messes on concrete cowhouse floors (therefore there's no sense in hosing the floor down, although water was laid on for that purpose), and lots of other won't-work stuff. In a phrase, the bunk has come my way, to be debunked after a certain amount of controversy, which usually ended in someone doing a bunk from my uncomplacent self.

Not all 'theory' is right, of course. Not all is practicable. Not all 'theory' comes out of intense and prolonged practice. When it does, we get a Rolls-Royce engine; a Mitchell Spitfire; a Ferguson hydraulic tractor; radium; prontosil; and the new strains of leafy grasses developed by Sir George Stapleton. And we get a revolutionary American who has written a book called *Plowman's Folly*,* in which he sets out to prove that the whole principle of plowing has been injurious to the human race.

Plowing in America has caused millions of acres of top-soil to be eroded by rains into rivers as silt, which in turn caused flooding and devastation in tens of thousands of square miles of the valley-lands. But that is only an indirect evil, declares revolutionary Mr Faulkner; adding that the devastating effect of plowing is to destroy the

*By Edward H. Faulkner. Published by Michael Joseph in the UK in 1945, as *Ploughman's Folly*.

cohesion of the earth-particles, thereby permitting loss of moisture, and a consequent crippled root-system of plants.

He has grown amazing crops without the use of the plow. He leaves the 'muck' on the surface. For the plow, he substitutes the disc harrow. On one field he grew rye, disked it in when green, leaving the 'trash' on top to rot and feed the surface roots of the succeeding crop, which, despite all the critics, was a bumper one. Setting out tomatoes, he rammed the earth hard where the plants were going, laid the roots on the rammed spot, covered them with soil, and left them. They outstripped plants set out in the ordinary way in both growth and yield.

The discs make a mulch of the 'green trash' and press it an inch or two into the earth; and that is the seed-bed ready, and the food of the crop to be. He has apparently succeeded as brilliantly as Mr Hosier, of Wiltshire, who first in England had the idea of folding cows on rape and turnips, taking the milking machine to them in the fold, leaving them out every day of the year to muck the land. In this way tuberculosis has disappeared and poor downland grows 14 sacks of wheat an acre.

Of course Mr Faulkner's idea of soil consolidation is not new. Our forefathers knew that wheat often grew better plants on headlands which had been 'jammed'. Also sheep on roots consolidated the soil, and afterwards a 'fleet' plowing of five inches, no more, was the rule for barley. Sometimes I think that the old-style farmers knew more than do modern farmers, for all their sacks of factory-made artificial dope called plant 'food'. Our forefathers knew the value of marl, of well-rotted muckheaps, of mud pulled from the dykes and set out with reeds and other litter in great heaps to heat and decompose and to come out into the tumbrils 'like black butter'. (Our forefathers, of course, were not blighted by the effects of international usury of the past fifty years.)

I have always wondered why the most successful crops grown in my six years on the farm have been grown on unplowed land. The first was of oats. We had a coomb or so in the drill left over, it was late on Sunday afternoon, getting chilly, and I was fed up and wanted to go home. What to do with them? They were mercury-dusted and no good for feed. Coming down by the wood I passed about an acre of cold old sticky land, on which vetches and winter oats had failed. Come on, I said, let's get rid of the oats on this. The soil was like putty, the shoe-coulters drew straight lines on it, about half an inch deep. Well, I said, let the birds take it, and if they get sick it's their lookout. Even as we left two cock pheasants walked out of the Fox Covert and began to pick up the oats.

No harrowing in, no rolling, just left like that. In August the oat-sheaves were a deep golden brown, very heavy in the head, a pleasing oily-glossy feel about them, very 'corny', over twenty sacks to the acre. The oats 'properly' drilled were not half as good.

The second astonishing crop arose out of land which was, I was told, a waste of time to cultivate. 'Nobody has grown a crop off there yet, you don't mind me telling you, do you? Don't let me interfere, but I've known this land many years, and no one has yet done anything with it.' I, however, am obstinate, and my idea was to loosen some of the accumulated leaf-mould in the woods with the hydraulic plow, and cart it on the slopes of the 'unkind old land'. This we did, meaning to plow it in; but it was late and already time to get on with spring drilling. Only when all the other fields were done did we come back to the heaps of leaf-mould and scatter them lightly (scarcely more than black pepper on a plate of food) on the four acres. It was a dry spring, and I knew that to plow then would be to turn up the yellowy soil dry as broken bits of dog-biscuit. Also, I didn't want the humus buried. I had the notion that to cultivate shallowly, hardly stirring the crust, to leave about an inch of loose soil on top, and then to drill oats and broadcast peas, was our only hope on this late April afternoon. Result, no thistles and a heavy yield of golden-brown oats and some useful peas.

There was a whitish chalky scald-patch at one end of the four acres, where rabbits sported, and where the barley of previous years had grown no higher than eleven inches, diminutive and sparse mouse-ear stuff. I left a few square yards of this scald land as it was; and spread the mould on the rest of it. Where no blackish 'pepper' of mould fell the oats were dwarfed; but alongside them, with roots absorbing the black specks of 'compost', grew thick oat-stalks five feet high.

Disc harrowing would have done even better than cultivating with duck-footed tines; less moisture would have been lost.

Some farmers, in the pre-eminent arable county of Norfolk, cultivate the plowed frost-tilth in the early spring, roll immediately, and follow the roll with the drill. Later, the heavy rib-roll goes over the springing corn, consolidating the land yet again, thus enabling the delicate fibrous rootlets of the corn to absorb the subsoil moisture drawn up by capillary attraction. Even so, I wonder to myself how many plows – evolved from the old apple-tree mould-board – will be in use in England in twenty years' time, now that the Victorian accumulations of gold, from the pickings of the rest of the world, are gone; now that we are a debtor-nation, and must live largely off our own soil, or die.

November 1, 1943

The Writer's Trade

I

A few months after the signing of the Treaty of Versailles, way back in those days when the war was over and immense hopes were in people's hearts (but little concerted will or energy to act on those hopes), I took one of my early nature essays to Sir Theodore Cook, then editor of *The Field*. It was called 'Spring in Windsor Great Park.' It was written after a walk there during an afternoon of quiet sunshine, in February, 1920. I carried on my arm an overcoat made out of an Army blanket; one of those lengths of Harris tweed which became blankets for the troops of the New Armies, in the hectic days of 1915.

The buds of the elms were breaking in a rufous haze; the song of the great titmouse was audible; the green woodpecker or gallypot was 'laughing' in the hazy distance. So eager was I for the Spring that I sat down then and there and wrote about it in prose that I thought would startle the world.

Such were my feelings, released after more than five years as a soldier; but when the kindly editor of *The Field* read my essay, and sent a brief criticism which was in effect a rejection, I was as downcast as I had been buoyant. One sentence alarmed and puzzled me. 'You should avoid clichés,' he wrote, after saying that there were signs in the essay which gave promise that I would, if I were prepared to work hard, eventually learn to be a writer.

What was a cliché? According to Chambers's Dictionary it was 'a stereotyped phrase.' After inquiry, I learned that a stereotyped phrase was one kept in type by a printer to save him picking it out, letter by letter, when type-setting. In a country newspaper, for instance, weddings and funerals were frequently reported, and so certain phrases were kept ready for use. 'The contracting parties were . . .' 'A very pretty wedding was solemnised at . . .' 'Among the

97

handsome presents were . . .' 'There were many floral tributes . . .' and so on, phrases to be set in use again and again, ready-made.

When it came to fiction writing, there were such clichés as: 'He stood rooted in horror to the ground;' 'The weather was beyond reproach;' 'The woodland was carpeted with bluebells;' 'The sun shone in a cloudless sky;' 'A cross marks the spot where the body was found;' 'A veritable hive of industry;' and so on and so forth. These then were clichés; and Sir Theodore Cook had advised me to take them out of my prose.

I had just finished my first novel, called *The Beautiful Years*, and I ran upstairs to my writing room (where I had a tame owl who lived in a corner cupboard) to look once again at its pages. Before, in reading them to myself, the door safely shut, I had quivered with secret joy that the pages were glowing with the very light of Nature, more real than the reality itself. But now, when I stared at the typed pages, I saw only cliché after cliché. The pages were dull and dead. The very first sentence, which when I had written it tremulously had brought back to me the windless, waveless blue of an early summer morning, seen from a headland high above the Atlantic, was a cliché. 'The weather was beyond reproach and the sun shone in a cloudless sky.' O horror! the book was all like that, even to the carpet of bluebells laid on the floor of the wood. Carpets! Hanging up in Hampton's windows! Men with aprons appearing out of a large van and laying down carpets of blue-bells! For days I was depressed, almost without hope. I even played a game of billiards in a pub. I was the family waster, who wouldn't work.

Failing at billiards, I started to cut out all clichés and to think out how to use words to make the scenes instantly visible to a strange reader, my new critical self. Thus I began my apprenticeship to the art of writing. Without that doleful period, without the salutary criticism from the kind editor, I might for years have persisted in associating my intense personal inner feelings with the words put outside on paper, thus continuing to write privately, as it were, and in this manner I might gradually have come to the bitter belief that the British public always neglected to appreciate original talent until it was too late.

Thinking and writing ready-made thoughts and ready-made phrases, I was no artist; I had yet to learn, by unlearning much that I had unconsciously absorbed from other people, from stunt news-papers, from dud politicians (who 'explored every avenue and left no stone unturned'). In other words, I had to find my true self, and begin again. It was a lonely and unhappy period; solitaries of olden time went into the wilderness to find the truth in themselves, and thus to true themselves up. It took seven years before I could sit down and re-create the reality of the life I had observed about me. Old-time acquaintances, when I met them again, remarked that I was an entirely different person, inferring that the change was not for the good. Some were still talking, in the same old beer-houses, about their literary careers, which had yet to start. They cursed the dud British public. Others, more elderly, were still talking in terms of the thought of 1914–18. This was painful, for I had by then come to believe that unless the entire thought of every human being changed, the same results from the same mental causes would occur again.

On my desk lie several bits of writing sent in for my opinion by various amateur scribes, some of them, perhaps, awaiting to hear the 'verdict' with an apprehension equal to my own when I dared to send 'Spring in Windsor Great Park' to the editor of *The Field* nearly a quarter of a century ago. Not all are young writers, however; two tell me they are established in business, and might they trespass on my valuable time to ask my opinion? (The businesses are not defined; they do not apparently include the use of stamped-addressed envelopes.) Another writes asking me to find him a cottage, so that he can begin his literary life; yet another (and this is interesting) tells me a few bare facts of an astonishing farming career of over fifty years, concerning 16 farms making up over 5,000 acres, adding that 'farming has been a good proposition all that time for me, no depression or fault-finding with the Government.' And last, streets ahead of them, comes *Hitler's Whistle*, a new book made up of journalistic bits and pieces by the famous author of *Farmer's Glory*. Art is long, time is short, newspaper columns are shorter, so those who have read so far must wait for further words on the above until next week.

November 8, 1943

II

The pages of writing sent to me for my opinion still lie on my desk. What can one say to the various amateur writers, and not hurt the pride of their various self-conceptions? Everyone has a picture of himself in his mind. Often it is a shock to find out what other people really think about ourselves. We judge ourselves often by our intentions, and by our better intentions, at that. Do we deceive ourselves? It is easier to deceive ourselves than to deceive other people.

Thus someone has sent me a description of a holiday, and asks my opinion on his essay or article. Obviously he thinks that he has conveyed the goodness of a recent holiday in words written on paper, for he sends them to me, for my opinion. In case I am in doubt, he encloses with the essay a letter from the editor of a well-known quarterly which deals with country matters. That editor has been, I can see, politely evasive. Owing to lack of space due to war restrictions, he regrets, etc.

> A fortnight later we arrived at a station somewhere in East Anglia, not nearly a thousand miles from a considerable town and not a hundred miles from the county border. Fields were aripening for harvest, birds (and planes) aflying, the sun shining, flowers blooming – and plenty of people being killed (in Russia at all events), as we made our voyage of discovery and finally arrived at our destination, and thereupon entered unknowingly the latter part of the 16th or 17th century, or was it the 15th? – we have not yet decided – but perhaps Mr. Wells' Time Machine can tell us.

Well, the editor certainly lacks space to print the above 100 words. Now, if our would-be writer regards his MSS as something to be cabled abroad, each word costing 5s., and he has only £6 to spend, and in 24 words he must convey the facts obscured in the above passage, then he would begin to understand the first problem of writing; which is to convey a factual picture to a stranger in the fewest, simplest words. The self-conception, the private writing which is self-enjoyed but unreadable by anyone else not of the intimate circle (and do they care?), has to be broken and cast away before any start at writing is made. Self-conception; not conceit, for the word 'conceit' has been debased, and is now a word of depreciation.

If one tries to make a truthful criticism of amateur writers, nearly always their pride is hurt. Writing, of course, is a trade or an art; proficiency only comes from endless pains and tenacity to learn, unlearn, discard, tear up, rewrite, recast, tear up, cross out, alter, begin again, scrap once more, to persevere through much self-dismay and feelings of hopelessness. It is like singing, or piano-playing, or designing aircraft, or surgery. I know a pianist who spends hours every day practising on a dummy piano, in silence, to keep his fingers supple. Or like being a film-star, a job which entails endless patience and power to endure innumerable rehearsals and retakes, hours of hanging about under staring lights and everything seeming hollow and empty. If you can project your inner self against all that nihilism, endure your emotion or spirit being wasted and yet summon all of yourself to do it over and over again, if you can do what you are told by the director and do it many times, and yet more times, and never reveal your weariness, then you may in time become that reliable actor called a star. The greater the glamour of the finished acting the greater the loss of vitality to the actor. What is left over for his private life often isn't worth having. So, with writing. You can't take a fine crop out of a field without the field's fertility losing by measure of the crop taken.

It is a problem for professional writers how to deal with the enthusiastic 'efforts' of amateur writers. The amateur's writing is still part of his personal emotions; and how can one criticise another's feelings?

Amateurs sometimes say: 'My writing is as good as So-and-So's, much better indeed, but I can't get it printed.' (One gentleman in the R.A.F. wrote that to me the other day.) But the amateur does not consider that So-and-So has, through years of professional work, made a name for himself. So-and-So's name has already made friends with many people, who know him through that name's work, and greet him as a sure friend, even if he has not much to say. But a stranger who has not much to say ... how do you react to him? You don't know him, and you honestly don't care anything about him. How can you, not knowing him? But a stranger who comes in and attracts you immediately by his interesting manner, who makes you feel at home in your own home, and you want him to stay longer and look for his next visit ... well, he is like the new writer editors are always hoping to find.

In writers we know and like, for their personality, we forgive much that is immediately observed as a fault in an unknown writer. Thus Mr A. G. Street, in his new book, *Hitler's Whistle* (which is what an old man called the air raid warning in his locality) uses clichés like 'the countryside has been a veritable hive of industry' to describe the corn harvest of August, 1939; but we are tolerant of this, for we already know him well by his broadcasts, his articles, and his books. Arthur Street is a personality: he can sneeze all through a broadcast, he can jumble up his words, he can even say, 'I'm a bit tired at the moment, mind if I have a snooze for a couple of minutes?' and we would wait by the loudspeaker, only too willing that our friend, whose West Country voice we know so well, should have a rest. If the Prime Minister, in a talk, were to growl *sotto voce*, 'Bring me another cigar,' or, 'Have you got a match?' we would feel honoured to share that detail of his intimate life. But when someone we don't know tells us that when recently he took a holiday not a thousand miles from an unknown somewhere and not a hundred from an undefined border, he unknowingly entered the latter part of the 16th, or was it the 17th century (no decision made) and perhaps an established author's fiction device might tell us, we don't honestly want to know whether it eventually turned out to be an Eskimo's igloo.

A. G. Street's book is made up of articles from farming and other journals. He calls it a diary, but it is not a real diary. It is a collection of weekly articles, broadcasts and other journalism covering three years of war. A diary would be very different; but I doubt if Street keeps one, apart from a technical farm diary. The style is the man; and here is the real Arthur Street, in this collection, the articulate, normally clever and observant English farmer, humorous and wise by experience. He is a 'safe' man; we trust him. He is neither a great stylist nor a great farmer; but there is only one like him in England, and that is himself. Read the book and you know the man. He has worked very hard, much harder than he knows; and in his auto-biography, *Wessex Wins*, he was inclined to deprecate his literary labours. But those who know the cost of writing, recognise this for the modesty of understatement. Writing is a whole-energy job; so is farming. Doing the two together is rather like trying to take two crops at the same time from the same field, year after year. When I saw him last, a week or two back, he was going away for a long rest to Wales, having to leave his Wiltshire farm and his literary work for awhile. A bare fallow, in fact, to restore fertility. Our best wishes to the author of *Farmer's Glory*, one of the best works of this century.

November 15, 1943

An Old Tractor

A farmer said to me, 'Let us have a laugh once in a while.' Very good idea, I thought, but why don't you make me laugh? As though in answer to my thought, he began to tell me a story of a tractor, a massive and old-fashioned affair which bore the appropriate name of Goliath.

I wish I could tell the story as he told it to me, for he used one or two Norfolk expressions which my ear-of-memory cannot recall; and I do not intend to compete with the fake-dialect style which sometimes shows itself in anonymous letters in local newspapers. So here goes, and if the laugh goes the wrong way, well, blame it on the old tractor.

A massive work of iron, steel, brass and copper had been standing for years in a hovel, providing a perch for hens, old sacks, rats and other 'warmin'. Although the Goliath had not moved for years it was in running order. Came the war and the need for extra plowing. A smallholder had an idea that he would like to plow, cultivate, harrow and roll his 7-acre pightle with the Goliath. His pightle, very neatly kept, with good hedges of a shrub he had planted and kept trimmed (in contrast to the hedges of broken sheep's hurdle and old iron bedsteads of some of his neighbours) was some miles away from where the Goliath stood. He did not like the idea of driving such a monster home, so he borrowed a pair of horses. Later that morning the new owner was to be seen seated on the Goliath, prepared for a mile or two of road-work, behind the chains pulled by the horses.

To drive a modern or even comparatively modern tractor is one thing; to drive a Goliath is another thing. It possessed, one must explain, a steering wheel of the worm type, like those on steam-traction engines. The driver had rapidly to circulate an iron wheel through many revolutions before the front wheels would respond. Such was the time-lag that often the horses, lugging the prehistoric iron monster, were proceeding along one plane while the Goliath moved along another. Thus it happened that progress was zig-zag until it ceased abruptly against a telegraph pole.

Set in motion once again, it plunged into a pond.

The new owner's troubles were by no means over when the Goliath was once more on firm land. When he got it home nobody could start it. It appeared that the monster responded to but one person, who had first driven it during the Napoleonic war (the last war but one, when British agriculture had the home market almost to itself). For more than a century the old Goliath had known the friendly clasp of one person on its huge double-handed crank, and so it would not respond to strangers, or 'foreigners', as they were called. When, therefore, one after another of a highly-interested group gathered round it on the pightle of its new owner, tried to swing it, simply nothing at all happened; though it was noticeable that Brylcreamed looks of manly hair, many inches long in the pre-war style, were soon falling all ways over glistening foreheads.

So the local strong man was called from his pint of XXXX ale in the Red Lion. What, start that little old totty thing? Baring massive arms to elbows, he gave a hitch to his plus-fours. Then with a lucky-charm blob of spittle well-rubbed into either horny palm, and a tightening of his lips, a settling straight of his cap-peak and a squirt from the quid of 'baccy in his cheek, the strong man gripped the double-handed crank, drew in a deep breath, and took a wrench at it, preparatory to whizzing it round; but hardly had he touched it when there was a puff of blue smoke, a great report, the whonk of a back-fire, and the strong man was observed to be ascending into the air, his eyes popping out of his head. He returned to earth, however, and to the Red Lion, and the ungrateful Goliath soon found that it had not a friend in the place.

Its new owner, however, was a man of tenacity. An SOS brought down the original engineer, who with a jerk of correctly applied foot-poundage evoked forth a stifling roar from his old pet. But alas, all was not plain sailing, or plowing, or whatever is the correct cliché, for the Goliath had been started while in gear, and now it was lumbering slowly forward, nor would it stop for all the shouts, but proceeded on its wobbling course right through a wooden shed wherein were potatoes, fertilisers, barley-seed, and many implements of honest hand-toil.

In vain its old driver, tears in his faithful eyes, pleaded for the good character of his pet. No modern horses for him, he cried; what was good enough for grandfather during the Wars of the Roses was good enough for him. In vain; the Goliath was disgraced. Had it not nearly knocked down a telegraph pole, submerged itself in a pond, made an honest pedestrian look like someone out of a low music hall trapeze act, and finally, ruined the entire premises of a farmstead? No more of the Goliath! However, it managed to plow three rounds with an old horse plow tied on behind before it sank finally into the earth, a damned thing.

Professor Krarkle, delving industriously into village trash dumps and behind butchers' yards for bits of teacup and bones and other exciting relics of an extinct civilisation, may come upon a sullen mass of iron pyrites in the subsoil of the age of Imbecilious Man; he may pronounce it to be one of the mythical steel monsters of the periodic International Trade Wars of the period, for what man of archaeology is infallible? How did the tank come there? On what tidal wave was it carried, all the way from the deserts of North Africa? There will be arguments in all the scientific papers. But I have left out one detail. The new owner, when he had got his machine home, and before the local strength was so sorely tried on that cranked handle, cleaned off every bit of oil and soil and painted the machine so carefully all over, that it would not have disgraced the Royal Academy. Alas, it blew oil, a veritable umbrella of oil, into the air with every rumble and snort of its engine; so great an umbrella of oil, indeed, that in that short journey it made to the wooden shed, every bit of paint was obscured, and it emerged from the other side its old black self again. Which may or may not be funny.

November 22, 1943

Seven Years After

It is pleasant to walk on English land that has been 'reclaimed'. The other afternoon I was standing below a wood on the slope of a field. When first I had walked over the field, seven years before to the day, it had been bleak and bare with old grey grass, from which arose thin black thistles and tiny brown stems of seeded docks. Rabbit burrows were marked in the wet expanse by heaps of chalk and scratchings in the yellow soil. It was a dreary scene on that November day of 1936. The three gateways of the sloping field were almost closed by brambles and elderberries – those weeds among trees. Of the gates nothing was left but sodden fragments of wood. The posts also had rotted and fallen. My companion, who was a professional valuer of land, turned to me as he marked the roll of the 25-inch Ordnance Survey map in his hand, and said, 'This isn't worth five shillings an acre.' He meant the annual rent; though I had an idea that he considered the land itself, which had a tithe on it of seven shillings an acre, was hardly worth buying even at that figure; for later on he advised strongly against the buying of the farm.

The other afternoon, when the field and I were seven years older, I looked around as I stood under the wood of pines and tall sycamore poles. I stood on the 'scald' patch, where seven years ago the rabbit-diggings had been numerous and white. Today there was sign of but one rabbit. In place of the short, thin, grey grass, which had never been grazed in years, and was thin because it was starved, a fine sturdy layer of rye-grass and clover was spreading in emerald lines through the stubble. A regular plant, as they say; and the finest clover plants of all were on the 'scald' patch. Down below were the meadows, with the thistles and rushes nearly extinct; two cuttings a year and close grazing had brought back the wild white clover and improved the texture of the pasture. How many tons of rotted mud and reeds from the grupps had we pulled out and carted uphill to the scald patch? We must have spread sixty tons to the acre. On

106

that patch our finest corn had stood during the past summer.

Both field and meadows looked young, fresh and healthy. Beyond the riverside carr I saw the pale blue of the sea. The sun was sinking towards the west; not yet sunset, but the trees, when I turned round again, were outlined black against the golden burnish of the sun shining through the wood. The air was mellow; it was marvellously clear; it was the air beloved of artists, the clear pure East Anglian air, and the colours of the trees in the carr beyond the meadows were the spirit of Cotman himself. Cotman, the artist whose works sold in his life-time for a few pence, saw and told the truth in paint; he had the pure vision of the clear and single-minded countryman.* And, standing there below the wood, my mind empty of material details, I felt myself identified, with startling clarity, with the pure colours of earth, sea and sky. It was as though I had seen them for the first time.

Were those colours to be seen on that day of November seven years ago? The colours were there, no doubt, but the spirit was not free to enter into them. The vibrations of colour were not received by the mind. The mind was not in tune with them. It was diminished by the weeds, the neglect, the desolation. On that day I was fearful, for I was about to enter into a laborious and, I was informed, a hopeless undertaking, which could end only in hurt to myself and to those with me.

I did not see the colours; I saw only the poor grass, the weeds, the brambles, the sodden and broken bits of wood that once had been gates – part of England in ruin.

I saw the system by which the home market had been denied to British farmers, because it was more profitable for town-minded financiers to lend money to backward countries, and to import cheap corn and meat as virtual interest on the money that was lent to those backward countries.

I saw the system, which had nearly ruined the land and the countryman, which had neglected the great Empire, which denied and frustrated all attempts to make any kind of resurgent change for the better, this system which lived by slumps and depressions, by the fall of one currency and the rise of another, which enriched the cunning few and impoverished the majority, culminating in a war to

---

*John Sell Cotman, 1782–1842. Born in Norwich, he was an intensely insular water-colourist who took his inspiration from the English countryside. Together with John Crome he remains the outstanding exponent of the Norwich School of landscape painters.

preserve itself – a war which, alas, alone would bring awakening, after great suffering, to the majority which did not know and which scarcely cared 'why things were the way they were.'

The valuer said, 'If you buy this land it will be against my strongest advice.' I said, 'I believe that a revival will come very soon; the writing is on the wall.' He said, 'It is not my business to be a prophet. I am dealing with things as they are today, not as they might be tomorrow.'

I saw the dole-queues in the towns – the heroes of tomorrow's battlefields – the dead who were yet alive – and I made up my mind to carry through my original purpose; to enter on a hopeless task and thus perhaps qualify myself to speak with authentic tones when the time came.

That was in 1936.

Since then, much has happened. Farmers have the home market. Prices are stable. Many farmers have paid off the mortgages on their land – the death engagements – only to mortgage the same lands again in order to pay the taxes which help to pay for the war machine. Many are worse off than before, though outwardly this may not be apparent. The farm labourer, too, is really no better off. Neither farmer nor labourer feels any true security. Wages may be double, prices may be stable; but there is no real security. During the war we accept the situation; but after the war?

The colours of the trees down by the carr, and the blue of the sea and the shape of the pines on the hill-crest are beautiful, for a moment; but until Truth comes to be the real motive force of human life, the spirit of beauty can be seen only in rare glimpses.

November 29, 1943

The Clodhoppers

I

The old saying, 'Break a field and make a man,' must have come about during the Napoleonic blockade of the Baltic, when England had to depend on her own wheat for bread. The price then went to about 160 shillings the quarter. It paid a man then to break up a field of pasture, and sow it with corn.

Recently there has been some correspondence in *The Times* about the wisdom, or the foolishness, of breaking up some old pastures which for a hundred years and more have fattened bullocks in spring and summer. Modern grasses, notably those bred by Sir George Stapleton in Wales, have more leaf and less stalk than the old. Some grow more quickly, others more slowly, thus providing a 'bite' both early and late in the year. There is little doubt but that grasses have been improved.

Another school of thought and experience declares that the old pastures – the best of the old pastures, which are grazed carefully, and kept almost like lawns – contain herbs (otherwise weeds) which the cattle select for eating as they feel the need for them; and that a layer of the new grasses is too strong, causing indigestion, or 'blowing', and 'scouring'. To this criticism yet others reply that new layers require as careful grazing as the old pastures, though for different reasons; and that once this new technique is understood the new pasture will be, because of its greater grass-virility, superior even to the old.

I come from a country which has a rainfall of 64 inches a year. It is famous for its Devonshire cream. Some fields let during the agricultural depression for £5 an acre solely for the grazing between early May and the end of September. Bullocks were wintered on those fields, given shelter in 'shippons' or sheds open to one side (away from the prevailing south-westerly gales), and in December and

January were given mangold to eat, strewn on the grass. Fine red bullocks they were, too, looking at a year old as big as many a two-year-old on the marshes of dry East England.

Devon is a warm county; the air is soft, and the speech is therefore soft; the rain falls and the sun shines, the Gulf Stream keeps the winters mild. The grass is green in the West when it is grey in the East. Like Ireland, it is a country of grazing beasts.

Before the war I used to get into my open car and return from the coast of Norfolk to the coast of Devon in a day, leaving the grey North Sea in the morning as the sun was rising, and coming to the emerald green fields of Devon, lying under the vast glory of an Atlantic sunset. Throughout the day, wherever I stopped, I heard the dialects varying with the soils; varying from the shrill, hard, clipped East Anglian to the rich burring voices of the rich-red soils of Somerset. And so to the ease of life in Devon, served by the slow and easy speech arising from fertile land, soil that was easy to plow, where a seed-bed could be made in any season except in heavy rain or frost.

In those pre-war days there was little plowing; half a million visitors every summer wanted half a million pounds and more of cream a week, and who was going to bother about growing oats or barley bringing in a gross return of £5 an acre, costing perhaps £4 10s. an acre to grow, when an acre of grass might yield £100 a year as a caravan site or £50 in milk and cream? And if you were particularly easy-going, and couldn't be bothered with milk or visitors, your 100-acre farm was looked after by one man, whose job it was to tend four-score bullocks which would fatten themselves merely by walking about and lying down.

Why bother to cut the thistles, even? Everyone had plenty of money. Missus took in visitors, maybe, at £4 4s. a week, and they were well satisified, for they came year after year. The place boomed. In the market town, on market day, the farmers did their business, arriving in smart new cars and sitting hours in the taverns, discussing everything except farming. The grass grew; that was their farming. They had no complaints. The harrows and the plows rusted in the corners of fields, hidden by nettles.

What a change today! During the 1943 harvest, which lasted until October, I saw sheaves of corn sprouting six inches out of the ear, in the swampy fields. The year before I saw hundreds of acres of corn laid flat on the ground; oats and barley, over-fed from the rich plowed turf, unable to stand up on the stalks, field upon field of laid corn which had to be cut by the scythe.

When I came to East Anglia seven years ago from that country of rains and salmon rivers, of deer and ravens and buzzards and steep oak-forested valley sides rising hundreds of feet above meadows, I made up my mind to turn all the grass of my Norfolk farm under the plow. If the meadows could be drained, or the tide kept back from the dykes, I would plow them too. As for the area of scruffy grass on the hills, grass which the original Danes and Vikings had probably trodden, that would be turned under in time. What, someone exclaimed, plow the best grass in the district, which the 'Ould Karnel' (a previous tenant) declared was the best bite for ewes in Norfolk? Plow that in? How about the steep sides of the hill? No tractor would go up there! Tractors would rear over and topple with the driver down to the bottom! What about the 'great old bull-thorns', who was going to cut them down?

The thorns came out, lugged by a traction-engine. The 50-ton steel cable broke nineteen times in the process. Some of them left their roots in the ground. We dragged out sixty-four trees, and then stopped; for it was time to drill, then it was time to hoe, then haysel, then harvest, and after that sugar beet. The old thorns lay on their sides during the next twelve months.

When we came to clear them the nettles were high around them. The wood was dry and hard for the axe. Bit by bit, however, the main branches were shredded, the small branches were burned, the limbs and trunks laid in heaps to be carted down to the circular saw. At last the hill was cleared, except for a few trees which the engine-driver, with his ragged lengths of cable tied together, dared not tackle. They might pull the engine over.

The hedges were spread over the grass. In one I found the remains of four barbed-wire fences, each a yard and more distant from its predecessor. Brambles were eight feet high, the homes of scores of rabbits. We cleared them by hand, but the roots stayed in the ground, most of them of the hard and sullen blackthorn. We burned the roots with fires which had to be doused with every black-out and re-lit the next day. Even so, the roots remained, and when we took the deep-digger plow to rip up the worst area by the hedges, for a summer fallow, we had to avoid most of them. The furrows left were very rough, heaps of bramble roots and lesser thorns. The soil under the turf looked dead and dry, as though no air nor rain had penetrated there for centuries.

December 6, 1943

II

Sometimes during the summer I used to walk up the hill, my feet pressing on the springy turf, in which grew rest-harrow, wild thyme, harebells, cowslips, and a thistle whose leaves pressed low on the grasses, in the shape of a star. Its flower was a purple-red, also pressing close on the sward. There were other thistles, too, the creeping thistle and an occasional tall annual spear-thistle. The creeping thistles were in colonies: even they found it hard to push their roots through the dense mat of roots of the various poor grasses. In the second year of war some tanks had come on the land, and cut up the turf, and in the early spring I had cultivated the tracks, leaving a loose tilth behind, on which a few seeds of trefoil and rye-grass had been broadcast, before being rolled, and forgotten. Along this tract of new land the thistles rose tall and thick, and the trefoil and rye-grass grew luxuriantly. That alone told me that the old worn-out turf should be plowed.

The fire-circles left by the burning of the deracinated thorns remained bare during the summer. Those headlands by the hedges, which had been roughly plowed after the brambles and blackthorns had been cleared, lay in sullen broken furrows. Our sheep, or what remained of the ewe-flock, had been sold a year previously; they had kept the grass pared in previous years. I wanted to begin plowing at once, but the hydraulic tractor had been broken, and sent away for repairs; and about this time also I had to go away, to hospital. So in June and July the hills were left to the winds and the flowers, to the kestrel who hovered over the plateau above for mice and beetles, and the village cats who prowled on the western slopes for rabbits.

There were about ten acres altogether, of varying slopes lying north, west, and south. An analysis of soil had been made, and the opinion given that the grass should be plowed in March and directly re-seeded on the upturned sod. The official trowel had discovered a light sandy soil, deficient in phosphate, and possibly able to support one crop of rye. This opinion had been given before the thorns had been wrenched out, with arboreal cries and groans, by the steel cable of the traction-engine. It was only when the trees were being dragged out by the roots that I saw they had been growing in a brownish-red medium clay, similar to that of the field over the eastern hedge. There was sand on the hills, for the rabbit burrows were yellow with it; and there was gravel also, for on the western slope lay a saucer-like depression which was obviously an old pit covered with grass.

I took a sharp spade and dug out a few feet of the turf. It was not easy, for the congested grasses and their roots were tough. It was curious how the soil was light only among the roots. As I broke it up in my fingers, seeing how it was a blackish mould and sand, it occurred to me that this ancient colony of grasses had, during the centuries, taken all the heart out of the soil, leaving only the sand. None of the original clay was left; only small grains of rock called sand amidst the grass and wreckage of centuries of dead roots. Under that layer, a fine medium soil was lying, ready to be enlivened by sun and air and rain. Plow and re-seed directly? And have the finest crop of thistles in the district? No. I would plow in the ordinary manner, leave a bare fallow to kill all the thistle roots, and drill with corn after a year.

The War Agricultural Committee were, as usual, pleasant and considerate in their attitude to this idea; and a suggestion was made, why not utilise the thistles for silage, or hay? Young thistles were not unpalatable; and if oats and peas were sown in early spring, they could be cut green in early June, after which the cultivators could keep the stubble stirred throughout the hot dry months of July, August and September, and thus kill the roots and fallow the earth in accordance with my original idea.

On Armistice Day the plowing began. The tractor was a 1937 Ferguson, with reconditioned engine and repaired hydraulic system. The plow was a double-furrow 10-inch. We opened the first top along the plateau, running from east to west, and returning west to east. That was uneventful going, although even in bottom gear the engine needed all its compression. It was Gulliver, among the Lilliputians; hundreds of roots were protesting and holding against the shear and lift of share and breast. Sometimes the furrow-wheel, with its iron spuds, turned thumpingly, as the resistance of an extraordinarily strong clump of rest-harrow roots held the plow shudderingly still. Rest-harrow: was that how the name first got about?

The tractor did not rest, a slight lift of the lever, and the hydraulic oil-pump lifted the plows; it went forward again, another touch of the lever setting the points deeper once more. I got off to look at those rest-harrow roots. Some were more than half an inch thick, dark like the roots of trees, surprisingly tough, going deep into the subsoil.

I saw that I could not hope to penetrate to the rich red clay at the first plowing. It took the engine all of its twenty synthetic horses to cut two furrows seven inches deep. The furrow-slices, too, were by no means tractable; I longed for mouldboards or breasts of the Olland shape, by which the slices would have been turned over nearly 180 degrees, laid flat. The furrow-slices often wavered, before deciding to sit upright, the grassy edge at right-angles to the earth. Never mind, I thought, snow and frost will subdue the old sod, and in the spring the new disc harrows will chop it up and press it down.

December 13, 1943

III

I wondered as I plowed the old turf of the hill, whether Dr Johnson, had he been with me that day, would have discovered an original meaning of a phrase often used among farmers, and labourers, to describe a stubborn object which temporarily frustrates their strength and ingenuity. Rest-harrow might, on account of its terrific roots, cause a pair of horses to stop, and the horseman with them, in sympathy; but an old sod was liable to do more things other than merely arrest the forward movement of a tractor. As I went on slowly up the slope, in bottom gear, peering backwards over my right shoulder, for the pleasure of watching the land being turned up and flopped over, always my hand was on the hydraulic lever, to raise the plows as the furrow-wheel began to 'scrap', or race in the furrow, because the pull of the turf was greater than the 2400-lb. pull of the tractor. Sometimes it seemed to scream: this was a stone caught between rear furrow-wheel and scraper. At other times it smouldered; smoke fumed in the furrow: this was a flint-and-steel spark igniting dry roots. But what was exasperating was to watch a strip of turf turning up behind me, hesitate, then with the aid of gravity unroll along its length, yard after yard, sometimes fifteen yards in length, and settle itself in the furrow again, grass side up once more.

It must be turned under, otherwise it would not only not rot, but live to grow with exuberance in the spring, stimulated by the nitrogen of snow and the oxygen of the sunlight.

I stopped the tractor, walked back and knelt down, tried in vain to heave over the dull resistance of many hundredweights of lifeless old sod. There the furrow-slice lay, ten inches by seven inches by fifty feet, a strip unbroken, marked by two parallel lines showing where the disc-coulters had cut the earth. The gulls which had been following the plowing, soaring and sweeping down on white narrow wings, with open red mouths, screaming for lug and wire-worm, now drifted in the upper air. I could not do anything about those stubborn furrows; I tried to replow them, coming back in reverse, then dropping the plow again and hoping to invert the slices on going forward once more. In vain; the slices curled up, reared high, doubled up and broke, choking coulter and mouldboard and frame, until I had to stop, to kick, wrench and push the heap apart.

What a mess, I thought; and remembered the injunction of the W.A.C. to plow in a 'husbandlike manner'. Well, some husbands kicked, wrenched, pushed and swore; so perhaps after all their injunction was being correctly carried out.

On the whole, it was not a bad job, and I don't think any other tractor, except a crawler, could have done it. Certainly not horses with an ordinary plow although a special match-plow might have turned a few furrows, until it was blunted and 'wrung'. The steep parts were the most difficult, for often the tractor was leaning over at an angle that made me wonder if it would topple and I should be underneath it; it was then that I longed for a Devon one-way plow and a pair of strong horses. There were rabbit warrens on the slope, too. I gave up when the off-wheel sank to the axle, lest we disappear altogether.

Avoiding the slope, I went round the base of the hill, thinking that the disc harrows would finish the work in spring, and anyway it wasn't practicable to expect a good crop the first year. The great thing was to rip up that moribund old turf.

While I was going slowly round, the gulls suddenly flew up, and I saw six small boys on the skyline immediately above me. One explained that they had been trying to reverse the sullen furrows; and might they follow behind, and push back the furrow before it made up its mind to turn the wrong way?

This was a fine game for them; and they fell on the unpatriotic turf with the eagerness of starlings, dropping on their knees and pushing and heaving with teeth clenched, man literally wrestling with brute Nature. After awhile it became somewhat arduous, so they turned it into a game, under the leader, whose job it was, apparently, to stand above and, with a wave of a stick, which was also a tommy-gun, to lead his men down to the assault of the backsliding furrow. The fun, of course, was in leaping down the furrows, all together, like a charge of the Home Guard at exercise early on a Sunday morning.

It was not long before hands and knees were grubby with soil; and the clodhoppers had invented other rules of the game, which took them from the wake of the tractor to the inside of a distant hen-house, which was their headquarters. The gulls, which had been waiting on above, came down once more and restarted their screams and scramble for worms, mice and insects.

The sun disappeared in the west, small and smoky. The air grew colder. Frost in the shade by the lower hedge began to look whiter. The engine seemed to be noisier. I began to feel that farming wasn't so interesting after all, and how much nicer to be writing beside a fire. One more round, I thought, before leaving the tractor by the hedge, water drained and cloth tied over it. The flights of starlings had gone across the sky; the gulls had left, too. Well, it was the last round, and now the mind must stop thinking, lest it get pessimistic. Go home, wash, change, and relax. Coming to the top again, I ran round 'empty' along the headland – which had been plowed in the summer, and was now a pleasing brown of half-rotted turf and broken tree-root – and set in along the last furrow. In front of me was a whiteness, where a long snake of turf had curled back; and stopping the tractor, I got off and went stiffly forward, to stand above a pair of delicate grey wings spread motionless on the frosting grass. One of the black-headed gulls, alighting and dipping for a worm, had been caught by the back-curling furrow. It must be suffocated, I thought, as I knelt to heave back the turf. It was heavy, and I felt tired, but at last I got it free, expecting the bird to be limp and crushed; but with a turn of its head and a feeble scream from its red mouth, it elbowed itself lightly into the air, and flew slowly away.

December 20, 1943

A Hero of Humanity

Is the power to understand others a gift or a curse? A few men and women are born on this earth with an intelligence and curiosity so sharp that lesser men say they have the gift of second sight. Certainly there are many recorded cases where a keen intelligence has brought little else but suffering to the possessor. The stake, the Cross, the cup of hemlock, are facts known to nearly all.

Yet the only hope of peace in the world lies in the development and use among all human beings of the gift (or curse) of sight, insight, imagination, intelligence – call it how you like! It is that gift which enables the possessor to see and understand many sides of a question. Most people see but one side, their own side. Their minds are a matrix of their experiences, which vary with each individual.

Today the world suffers because in so few people has imagination been developed. Shocking things are done by men to men; similar acts are done in retaliation. The air is full of special pleading called propaganda. Justice in one man's conception is bitterly resented as social injustice by another. One of the great revolutionary thinkers (and creators) of the 20th century wrote that when he listened to Beethoven he wanted to stroke people's heads – until he remembered that heads had to be split in order that all people in the future might enjoy Beethoven.

Another great revolutionary, a hero to millions and an unspeakable villain to millions of others, began to break the heads of those who would split heads in order that Beethoven might be listened to with pleasing emotions. This revolutionary also worked to create a new system by which all might enjoy Beethoven.

Beethoven himself lived with great courage and immense despair, fighting the darkness in men's minds in the imaginative realms of his music, creating sweetness and light in the garret where he lived and suffered and died alone.

The revolutionary of the 'teens and 'twenties, the splitter of heads,

117

died and was embalmed. Millions have marched by his tomb in reverence and inspiration. Millions of others were not enabled to pay their tribute, as their heads had been split meanwhile. All in the good cause, so to speak.

Meanwhile the second revolutionary, who has seen only danger, and corruption of all that Beethoven stood for in the ideas of the first revolutionary, sets out to destroy those ideas once and for all; in order that Beethoven may be listened to without economic or political interruption for a thousand years.

Thus both halves of the world fight each other for freedom to listen, without economic fear or want, to Beethoven. Both sides fight for civilisation. The noise is terrific – the darkness-noise that Beethoven triumphed over in his sublime imagination.

The machine of civilisation breaks down every quarter of a century; that is evident. There is no need to be personal in a philosophical review of these tragic and heroic times. Conrad once wrote that every great work of literature could be summed up in one sentence, 'They were born; they suffered; they died.'

Could the present war have been averted? Many men tried to avert it, each in his different way. It is probably true to say that most men of responsibility in most countries tried to prevent the war happening; while by their very acts they also helped to bring it about.

Determination to make something new always creates opposition, because the making of the new involves the remaking of the old; and the old wishes to remain as it is, or as it was. If determination persists, opposition hardens; and in the final result the irresistible force meets the immovable object. The rock becomes flame; the ploughshare is beaten into the sword. The bitter struggle for freedom without which no war would ever be started, begins; continues; and ends.

Is this the natural scheme of things? Is there no hope in the dreams of the visionaries, both active and inactive, that one day Beethoven – and all the world of art and beauty and culture of which Beethoven was one of many prophets and creators – may be the equal of all men, because all men share a greater imagination and understanding?

The supreme Prophet of the world's eventual salvation was born one thousand nine hundred and forty-three years ago. I have just been celebrating His birthday. The capital H is used in respect to His genius, to that supreme quality of imagination and vision which brought the bearer of those gifts to a very high place in the esteem and wonder of some of his contemporaries; which also created in established or old minds a fury which brought Him to criminal execution in public.

Mr Bernard Shaw, a genius of this modern age, has written that if Jesus of Nazareth (that little village which didn't think much of its celebrity during His lifetime) had tried to force through a new way of life or system He might have gone down in history as 'a bloody-minded tyrant.' But Jesus saw all sides of a question, at least in the later years of His life, and this understanding was its own innocence. To understand all is to forgive all; to give way. If one knows the sincere motives of one's opponents, can one counter them? One's neighbour is oneself; his hopes are one's own. Break his head, and his brother will break your head. That is no good at all.

Beethoven, friendless and alone, dies in his garret, dies shaking his fist at the darkness of an ongathering storm.

Mobs shouting for this or that hanging, or for this or that head to roll in the sand, tell us that we have not yet learnt to perceive, and then to tell, the truth of human understanding. We live in an age of supreme mental suffering; yet our hope lives that those to follow after may live the happier for it; that they may see plain, and hear joyfully.

December 28, 1943

Finance and Farming

M r Hudson, as many know, is the Minister of Agriculture; and, as many do not know, the Minister of Agriculture has only limited powers. He has to take his orders from the Cabinet; and the Cabinet, broadly speaking, has to take its orders from the Financial System which is also called Great Britain.

This Financial System is all of us and everything about us. It is neither the Banks, nor the great Insurance Companies, nor Investment Corporations and Trusts, nor the Jews, Big Business, Stock Exchange, Wall Street, Vested Interests, etc., but it is all these things together, and it rules Parliament, and all but the crank minority political associations. The Government is its agent. At the moment the Government has a limited power to control financial operations. For example, I am not allowed to invest money in German armament concerns; nor are you allowed to have any money in the United States without telling the Government. If I try nowadays to invest my £10 savings in the Skoda works, I am likely to be shot in the Tower, or perhaps hanged at Pentonville, as a traitor. If you don't declare your holding of dollars in the United States, and Treasury officials find out, you are likely to be fined thrice the amount of money you had there, as well as lose the original sum. Also, you will be publicised in the newspapers as unpatriotic.

Before the war you or I might invest our money where we liked, in Germany, Japan, India, Ireland, the United States, Poland; or even in the firework industry of Tierra del Fuego. Nobody could stop me or you being a financial wizard. If you were very rich, say the head executive of a vast financial concern, you might perhaps have big holdings in Poland or Middle Europe, or South America. By big holdings is meant money invested in loans, covering industries in coal, steel, or agricultural mortgage. Of course, interest would be payable on these loans, else you wouldn't invest in them; and the usual way of taking interest was in importing the goods those countries produce. Your investments would help employment in those foreign countries; the more work, the greater the value of your investments, and the greater your profits. You would have a lot of goods to dispose of from those countries, and those goods would virtually be interest on your and your shareholders' financial holdings. Where else but in Britain would those goods be sold, to turn them into cash, with which to pay the dividends of your shareholders? At least, the bulk of them would go to Britain.

Thus, in the pre-war days, which today we say were not good enough, from South America came frozen beef and maize and other grain; from Central Europe came barley, turkeys at Christmas, glass, boots, and many other things. Coal from the Polish mines, financed with British capital, sold cheaper abroad than Welsh coal, because the Polish miners received only 14s. a week before the war. The strength of Great Britain was said to be in her Great Financial Interests, which ruled the land, the people, and their elected representatives in Parliament and so in the Government.

Bearing this fundamental truth in mind, the reason why agricultural prices flopped after the war of 1914–1918 is plain and simple. If British farmers retained the British (i.e. Home) market, then the cheap food from abroad would have been excluded, or most of it. If this food was not imported, trade would suffer; financial investments would suffer. And in peace time financial interests can kick out any Government which does not put those financial interests first. Parliament does not rule in peace time; the Government does not rule. The Money Power rules; the system which you and I help to maintain by saving money and investing it in what we hope will be a profitable investment, anywhere in the world.

During the war, you cannot invest your money abroad; you are urged, even compelled, to use it for the good of your country. Everyone, even the profiteer, verbally agrees with that in war-time; the actual land and the actual people come first before any foreigners. Anyone asking a bomber pilot to drop a bundle of British notes earned in, say, aerodrome work, over Berlin, with a written request that the cash be invested in German Bonds, would be told not to be so silly. You must wait until the war is over; then you may be able to do it, through your local bank in the ordinary way.

We haven't forgotten Mr Hudson, the Minister of Agriculture with very limited powers. We wish to make it quite clear that under the Money System which has been built up during the centuries, international trade has grown and become complicated and that the top-dog or top-producer for a long period was industrialised Britain, whose factories supplied the world and whose ships carried the goods over the Seven Seas.

Of course, when we had taught other countries to use the machinery we had sold them, they used it, and made what we had made exclusively before we had sold them the machinery. They became our rivals. If Lancashire could make a cotton towel in 1896 for 2d., while paying 18s. a week to a full-time skilled man, those 'backward' countries could make the same towel for ½d., since their full-time skilled man received only 2s. 8d. a week. Under Free Trade this sheet came in, and your grandfather bought it and the Lancashire mill-hands began to feel the cold draught; and after another decade or two, the full-time skilled man up there was turned off, and had no money to take home at all. His cousin, coming to find work after being turned off from the farm which lost money year after year because the market was gone for its products, joined him in the search for work.

Is it too late now for Great Britain to put its land and people first; and raise the standard of life in those vast territories of the British Empire, while keeping every factory and home working full-time, by investing all its money only within the spaces of the Empire? There were enough raw materials in the Empire to supply all the wants of Great Britain; and enough technicians in Great Britain to equip the people of the Empire with all they wanted. But that was the dream of a few cranks.

If after the war farming prices drop and the fields tumble down to weeds again, it will not be Mr Hudson's fault. He has done his job to the full extent of his powers, which are powers limited to him by the Government; and the Government's powers are limited, not by the will of the people as is loosely supposed, but by the paramount power of the Financial System.

January 3, 1944

Local Farming Profits

The 'Letters to the Editor' column of this newspaper has printed recently some facts or fantasies or opinions about farming profits. One anonymous writer has declared that he made over £20 an acre profit last year, after paying £4 a week wages to his men.

As a small farmer myself, this of course interests me; but I cannot help wondering why the successful smallholder did not give, or allow, his name and address to be published. Was it that he did not, after all, pay his men £4 a week, but instead, they averaged this (as a great many do) and more during periods of hoeing, harvesting and sugar beet lifting? On my farm this year the men averaged £1 a day for lifting – and, owing to a poor crop, the farmer's expenses were just covered by his receipts!

I met a man last week who told me that he farms a smallholding of considerably less than 50 acres in North Norfolk, and that he made over £800 profit last year. I am, of course, not at liberty to give his name; it was a private conversation. Nor can I say how he made that sum; but it was due to judgement in buying stock, combined with the unusually dry and frostless open winter, which provided him with plenty of feed. (The very weather conditions that spoiled my sugar beet the following season!) He employs one man, and is, I should judge from his easy and knowledgeable manner, a good employer. He is an ex-soldier of the last war; and so cannot be condemned by some anonymous objector for living on the fat while soldiers live on the lean.

I must confess that his revelation of a profit of over £16 an acre filled me, when I thought of my own farm accounts, with a conviction that I was inefficient and lazy. And, bearing in mind the virile letter from a correspondent of Great Massingham, published in this paper last Friday, in which the writer wishes good-luck to all efficient smallholders, who 'clean and store implements ready for immediate use,' my self-searching was again directed to a review of my past financial year.

I farm 235 acres. Of these, 35 are woodland, and therefore do not come into the farm business except that their reserves of compost have been carted out at times to improve scald patches of arable; and the resulting corn more than paid the cost of digging, carting and spreading. That leaves 200 acres, of which 80 are grass today. We have plowed 15 acres of our rough grass, thus making up our arable to 120 acres, of mixed soils, ranging from light sand (about three acres) to sticky brown clay, or loam.

I employ my son, aged nearly 18; an old age pensioner (paid full wages); a man of 32; a youth of 18, with charge of all live-stock; a pensioned soldier of 1914–18, who was badly wounded; and another man who has recently joined us. Last year we had a girl, who worked well, in place of the new man.

Our sales are from corn, sugar beet and livestock. We do not sell milk, but rear heifer calves. The farm was in poor shape when I took it over, after about twenty years of neglect. Three years ago it was ranked as an 'A' farm; though when I heard this I wondered what a 'C' farm must be like.

The wages for the past year, ending at Michaelmas, 1943, were £1,000. Other expenses were about £1,000. These included fertilisers, £227 (a large item, including 100 tons of pressed sewage to help restore a field unmucked for many years); seeds, £47; drainage rates, insurance, rating services, £64; blacksmith, veterinary, etc., £70; fuel, £138; tractor repairs (Ferguson hydraulic housing was smashed and engine reconditioned after five years' hard work), £150; tractor spares (including another broken Ferguson bought for spares), £96.

Receipts were: Livestock, £690; corn, £1,618; sugar beet (after deducting labour of lift-top and haulage to factory), £370.

Taking the expenses at, roughly, £2,000, and the receipts at £2,700, a difference of £700 is left.

Before a profit can be assessed, however, the valuation at the beginning of the year has to be offset against the valuation at the end of the year. This is where things do not look so good.

The valuation at Michaelmas, 1942, was £3,338. At Michaelmas, 1943, it was £1,437.

When I looked at the differences my heart sank; until I remembered that whereas the valuation of 1942 included £1,550 of corn unthreshed, there was no corn unthreshed by valuation 1943.

In assessing a profit, valuation 1942 has to be added to the expenses in the year; while valuation 1943 has to be added to the sales. And the sales have to include, of course, the cash for corn sold during 1943, which is the corn in the 1942 valuation, £1,550.

I hope this is not too complicated; but in effect it means that, when I have allowed for rent (£105) and depreciation (£182) about £170 is left as a net profit.

On our farm we care for, and constantly ask for, and indeed only live for, neatness, efficiency, cleanliness. As it is apparently an affront to ask for the removal of horse-dung from our new and costly roads, we send the children to do it after school. We grease plows after use, we send one or another of our sons to work off the rust with a broken scythe-rub, and leave the plow-breast oiled. We try and keep our sacks in proper rows in the barn, away from rats; barley sacks, oats sacks, meal sacks, all in different neat piles. Why not? Aren't we struggling for a better world? We even grease the hanging-irons of gates; we cut weeds twice a year on meadows (sons do it on holidays, Saturdays and Sundays if need be); we wash our hands before milking, and we hose (after five years of vain pleading) the cowhouse afterwards; we take great care over all cultivations; and we have found that the hardest part of farming is in the attempt to persuade the liberty-loving Briton to do likewise.

Our beet crop was an awful flop, due to the small back-end rainfall. I plowed the field deep and very carefully; I plowed it myself, once all night by moonlight, before Christmas, to be in time for the frost – which never came. Only light rains fell the following spring and summer. The crop averaged only seven tons an acre; we hoped on this, our best field, for fourteen or fifteen. Our barley was all fine malting samples, as it has been for many years. It averaged ten sacks each acre. Our livestock were badly served in 1942; the valuation suffers thereby. Judged solely by the cornfields, we took a profit of over £20 an acre; but the farm profit works out, including the meadows but not the woods, at under £2 an acre. And my real name is

Henry Williamson.

January 10, 1944

January 12, 1944

Sir – In my account of farming profits published in your paper of Monday last there was a misprint and an omission, and perhaps you will allow me to correct these. 'Rating services' should be ratin services. We found this method obliterated all the rats in a very short time. The omission was over the rusty plows. I could never persuade my teamman to grease his horse-plow after use – 'no one else does it round about' was the invariable excuse. In the end I had to do it myself, or send a son to do it. There was, of course, much dissension over this and scores of other similar omissions.

Today our plow-breasts shine all the time thanks to our tractor-driver, a young man of 17 years of age. – Yours faithfully,

Henry Williamson.

Literary Diversion

I

Just as the actor sometimes goes to see a play, to watch other actors at work, so occasionally an author reads a book. Does this sound extraordinary? It is no more extraordinary than a village rag, bone and scrap metal man stopping to glance at the dumps, if any, of his professional rival.

Literary critics are sometimes accused of not reading the books sent to them for review. Of course they don't always read them all through. Why should they? Does the bullock-grader under the Food Minister have to eat all of a bullock in order to find out if it is likely to be a nice young fat beast, or merely a poor old cow sent in after sixty or seventy years' service in the dark and unwashed milk shed of some village technician?

Before me lie four new books. Three of them, which I will deal with here, were bought by myself at the bookshop. The fourth was sent by the publishers, as it contains a few pages written by myself. Here are the titles, publishers, prices:

The End in Africa, by Alan Moorehead (Hamilton, 10/6).

Inland Farm, by R. M. Lockley (Witherby 10/-).

Rural Amateur, by Clifford Hornby (Collins, 8/6).

Countryside Mood, by Adrian Bell, H. J. Massingham, J. Wentworth Day, Frances Pitt, S. L. Bensusan, Lord Mottistone, etc. (Blandford Press, 10/6).

The book I enjoyed reading all through was Moorehead's *The End in Africa*. His story is balanced, vivid, authentic, and any combatant member of the B.N.A.F., or its rival the Afrika Korps, in hospital or internment camp, who could read English and was not too badly hurt, would be able to finish it. This is a compliment to Alan Moorehead's energy, ability, and lack of propaganda-mentality, otherwise preju-

127

dice. He tries always to write down the facts; his own opinions are not obtruded. Read this extract from Chapter 16, laconically called 'Longstop':

> The officer himself was very tired. He had been in the line for a week, and during the previous night some of his men had just fallen on the ground and cried. They cried because they had no strength any more, not even the strength to stand up. They had continued without sleep for two days under the compulsion of their brains and beyond the point where the body will normally function. But now, when their minds would not work any more, they discovered that the strength had already gone out of their bodies and that, in fact, they had no control of anything any more, not even of tears. The tears came quite involuntarily and without any sense of relief because the body was incapable of feeling anything any more, and what became of the body now was of no consequence. And so they had lain about the hill for an hour or two in a stupor. The cold and the dew bit into them through the night and brought them back to consciousness.

Obviously, Mr Moorehead has read his Hemingway; the above passage is derivative from the style of the author of *For Whom the Bells Tolls*. Mr Moorehead was not in the attack on Longstop Hill (which was not so bad as an attack on the Somme or so terrible as Passchendaele, because neither the mud nor the wet nor the frustrated immobility of Passchendaele has yet been equalled in this war) and his rendering of the soldier's reaction is as near as a non-combatant may get to the nervous reality of direct assault, counter-attack and prolonged shock-stimulation. Until the war is over, and some young sensitive ex-soldier turns poet or author, the war correspondent's interpretation will have to serve. When he reports what he has experienced, Mr Moorehead wins our full approval. (Of course, he cannot, during a war, describe all human details.)

> A profusion of things lay about all the way up the trench – empty cigarette packets, both British and German, water-bottles and hand grenades, half-used boxes of cartridges, German steel helmets, bits of note paper, discarded packs and torn pieces of clothing . . . There were several old London papers lying about. One, the *Daily Mirror*, had its last page turned upward and its thick headline read: ' "No more wars after this," says Eden.'
> Seeing me look at it the soldier on the end of the trench said bitterly, 'They said the last war was going to end all wars. I reckon this war is supposed to start them all again.' The others in the trench laughed

shortly and one or two of them made some retort. The men had greeted us with interest, but without enthusiasm. When they read the war correspondents' badges on our shoulders they were full of questions and derisive comments ... They were hostile, bitter and contemptuous. Every second word was an adjective I have not quoted here, and they repeated it *ad nauseam*. They felt they were a minority that was being ordered to die (a third of them had been killed or wounded during the night) so that a civilian majority could sit back at home and enjoy life ... The real degrading nature of war is not understood by the public at home, and it can never be understood by anyone who has not spent months in the trenches or in the air or at sea. More than half the Army do not know what it is, because they have not been in the trenches. Only a tiny proportion, one-fifth of the race perhaps, know what it is, and it is an experience that sets them apart from other people.

There we have the essence of the truth in the last line: that the sensitive, otherwise intelligent, survivors of the four million British casualties of World War I were unable to put over to the unregenerate and unawakened majority at home. Wherefore World War II; and World War III, unless the young and battle-purged soldiers make the peace.

January 17, 1944

II

After *The End in Africa* I took up Mr R. M. Lockley's story of how he tried to work a forsaken Welsh farm of poor land by the sea. He starts, as many others have started, with such appalling handicaps; everything must be right, work all day and half the night, urging others to feel and do likewise (which they don't feel and don't do) and coming to realise (until experience dissolves this initial view) that apathy and red tape are the greatest obstacles to *getting on with it*.

The old rook, white-faced with much corn and wireworm grubbing, waiting out of gunshot for the corn-drill to move off the field, caws derisively to all pioneers, '*Yer'll larn, yer'll larn!*'

In Mr. Lockley's *ménage* there is someone who looks like being a meat-for-manners man, a real 'old sweat', called the Baron. Whenever the Baron enters the story the reader is glad. He has done everything everywhere, it appears, and now on the staff of Inland

Farm he is odd-job and handyman, not forgetting the ferrets. Of these attractive little creatures he managed, with the help of their parents, to breed thirty-four; and what is more, he sold all of them for fifteen shillings each. The Baron was apparently well satisfied; but the farmer, lord of all, writes:

> They consumed about £1 of rabbits each week and were definitely not a business proposition. I encouraged the Baron to sell off his families of ferrets as soon as they were grown enough . . . He pocketed the money as his perquisite, and I swallowed the loss gladly.

Reading that chapter on Christmas Day, while my farm could go to Halifax for all I cared, I got a good laugh out of that. The operative word, as 'Beachcomber' would say, is 'gladly'. Mr Lockley apparently did a lot of things in the glad manner. He and Mr Leo Walmsley, the Yorkshire author of *Three Fevers*, who went to stay with him on the old farm with wife and large family, and helped him with much good advice of how to use tools, etc., particularly in the building of a hen-house, of which a photograph of Work in Progress is stuck in the book. The author of *Three Fevers* moved on, and perhaps one day we shall have another book from him, *The Fourth Fever*, telling us his experiences inside that hen-house, with an essay on the right way to hold a hammer.*

Some of Mr Lockley's 'fans' make the journey to see him, to tell him how much they like his books, and to bask in the rural scene, etc.

> Those who could not jump on the tractor or stand on the footboard of the combine drill with me were left standing in the yard, admiring, wondering, or cursing.

Farmers, rarely out of trouble themselves, like to read about other farmers' muddles (it makes them feel not so bad themselves) and so this book was especially readable at Christmas.

Rocks lie sometimes four inches under the soil of the fields of Inland Farm; and Mr Lockley had, apparently, lots of fun plowing with a W.A.C. tractor. How very agriculturally English was that scene on the base of a Welsh shale-stone promontory!

> Battered and neglected by a dozen contractors, it had been left at the nearest depot in despair by the last user. Many nuts, bolts, nipples and fittings were missing. The gear lever had lost its retaining spring and

---

**Three Fevers was published by Cape in 1932. In 1935 it was released as *Turn of the Tide*, the first film made by J. Arthur Rank.

nob, and it was only by a conjuring trick learnt from bitter experience that we eventually achieved the correct position of the gears.

The air conductor pipe was loose and vacillated so much that when it came to rest on the mudguard we lashed it there, as the safest place for it. When at least we got the engine started the exhaust pipe fell off. These were minor difficulties which did not dishearten me so much as the absence of greasing nipples. These had been stolen, making it impossible for me to service adequately the steering mechanism, with the result that this was stiff and almost dangerous. Also, as soon as we got on the road, the big near-side driving wheel showed every sign of coming off.

In fact it was in fairly sound condition; for at least it would move! The Baron put it in order, with Mr Lockley's help (or was it the other way round?). And when it went away it was okay; but the next borrower could do nothing with Dora, as they had affectionately come to know the dear old machine. He could not get her out of gear. However, it was not all like that. There was one occasion when the neighbours gathered to inspect Mr Lockley's work and, he tells us, to praise his courage with three hearty cheers. When he first started they came to help him, too, with plow-teams and plows, and their wives came to help Mrs Lockley get the house in order.

After the purgative realities of North Africa and the 'hard graft' of West Wales, one turns to the quiet and candle-lit undertones of the *Rural Amateur*. Mr Clifford Hornby tells us quietly, almost subduedly, of the realities of the life of a town-bred boy who always loved the country, and wild birds in particular, but whose way of livelihood kept him generally to bricks-and-mortar, otherwise urban existence. The narrative begins with his tame Spanish mice at school, which escape, overrun the perfects' room and are trapped by them, while he dares not claim them, but grieves alone.

Mr Hornby, who left school in the 'twenties, was a cameraman for the films, and before World War II he travelled about the earth, using 'stock' to get material for back-projection shots of films. He made friends with Captain Knight, the falconer and lecturer, and spent many happy hours with him and his nephew, Esmond Knight, the actor. They flew their tame hawks at rooks on Salisbury Plain, and sought eyesses at Lundy and elsewhere. The eyesses are the young peregrine falcons, which are taken as fledgelings from their ancestral eyries, usually on a ledge down some precipitous headland by the sea. Brought up in a 'mews', the powers of flight of the peregrines are small and weak compared with the wild strong birds. Mr Hornby describes a flight at a crow, which ended soon in both falcon and crow gaping exhaustingly on the grass. Esmond Knight once declared that the speed in flight of the tame peregrine is not more than 50 mph; the wild bird is capable of 'stooping' at nearly 200 mph in its native airs.

January 24, 1944

Herefordshire Hops

Wanting a clear space of time to revise a book, I went the other day to a part of England that I had not visited before, except to motor through its red clay arable fields in peace-time, on my way from Devon to Scotland. The county was Herefordshire, and my host was a farmer. I spent most of the day in writing, and at night we sat round his fire and talked of various things, including farming.

He was a man in whose veins ran the blood of many farming ancestors. The county was famous, among other things, for its big white-faced red-bodied beef cattle. I saw some in his fold; we would call it yard in East Anglia. He had 25 cows, and each cow was rearing its own calf. The calf was on the cow for nine months, when it was weaned, usually at about 6 cwt in weight. The weaned calves were fed on hay and mangolds and bean-meal until the grass was ready for them; then they grazed until the following winter, when they came in for fattening. After a winter in the fold again, each bullock was expected to weigh 13–14 cwt at an age of 28 months, when it went to the butcher.

For this herd, of 25 cows, their calves, and the bullocks being fattened, my host grew 20 acres of mangolds, 20 acres of beans, and, of course, enough hay from one-year leys. The rest of the arable was potatoes (grown because he was ordered to grow them in war-time), wheat and oats; but the farm was centred on the main crop, 50 acres of hops. The hops *were* the farm, and the growing and harvesting of them was a chronic source of worry to the farmer.

He employed eight men in normal times, three of them being in the folds or yards while the cattle were not out to grass. But for hop harvest he had four hundred extra hands and, what is more, he had to provide a habitation for them on his farm premises!

The four hundred came from South Wales. Then the fun on the farm began! He grew no swedes, for the simple reason that if he did none would be left for his cattle. About three to four of his ten acres

133

of potatoes were inevitably swiped by the pickers. He expected it. He expected also to lose all his wooden gates for firing. Any implement visible was liable to be the target of the Celtic boys, who still carried on the technique of the Stone Age. Once he had a tractor standing for an hour by the premises; at the end of the hour its plugs were shattered, their leads pulled off, the engine oil run out, also the water, and there were dents in its radiator and tank. After this, the boys had tried to start the weird machine; sign, possibly, of the general public's war-time interest in agriculture.

Before the four hundred arrived, to live in the barns, sheds, folds and outhouses, these premises were inspected by the Health Officer. He had to approve the quality of blankets, the white-washing of the walls, the cleanliness of the straw for bedding. This official also came when the four hundred were in action; and the farmer was responsible for all sanitary conditions while they were there. In addition, this agricultural Solomon had to settle family feuds, to plead for his old foreman, who was inevitably, and every day, accused of marking up short weight (for the hops were picked and delivered at piece rates) and of generally trying to cheat the pickers. He was liable at any time of the day or night during the harvest to act as midwife, bouncer, G-man, fireman, policeman, doctor, lawyer and flying squad. This, in addition to supervising the drying of the hops in the great kilns, where blasts of hot air from coal furnaces were rushed up by means of fans driven by Diesel engines. He had to attend to breakdowns. The hops were dried in shifts, and the drying never stopped during the 24 hours. His eight regular men received up to £10 a week during this time, and his foreman dryer got £15 a week. They burned 100 tons of coal in the furnaces.

Before the harvest, the hops in the yard – they received intensive cultivation, and lasted about 20 years as plants in rows – needed careful and perpetual attention. Green fly might easily ruin them in a few days. Nicotine powder at £95 a ton had to be blown on the green fly when it appeared, always at night, when it was damp. Sometimes six sprayings a year had to be given, two tons each spraying for the 50 acres. Artificials were not good for the plants; bone meal, potash and cattle dung was used.

In a good season the farmer might get 15 cwt an acre of hops. The price received was £16 10s. a cwt. It was a guaranteed market, also a closed market, by law. Even before the war only a certain acreage of hops could be grown. A newcomer could grow as many hops as he liked, of course, but he could not sell them. The Government had arranged this with growers and brewers.

When the hops were finished, the farmer then had the normal corn harvest to contend with, and his troubles were over, save for the ordinary little bothers of arable farming, until the next year. But he spent the interval (so far as I could see) in dreading the next picking. His wife told me he had never read a book. I asked him what he did with his evenings. He told me he sat and ruminated about the next picking.

January 31, 1944.

Ownership of Land

Sir Richard Acland, the West Country squire who has given his two estates to the National Trust, has done a wiser thing than some may suppose. The ownership of land today carries burdens and obligations which are not generally understood or realised.

Few people who do not know what ownership of a large estate entails, have any sympathy with a landlord. To some he is a villain, who lives on the fat of the land, enjoying an easy life without doing any work. These critics point to cottages on his estate, little buildings which are as damp, dark and inconvenient as they were three hundred years ago. I speak of the days before the war, of course, for since the war we have a Government which has the power to control land, money, and men alike. The Government today can dispossess a landlord of his house and fields at fourteen days' notice if that land is not being used in the national interest, which means not being used as directed by a group of Government officials. Personally, I welcome such national power of control, and for some years before the war had worked for it to come about in peace-time.

By giving his large family estate in Devon and Somerset to the National Trust, Sir Richard Acland – whose family has been landlords for hundreds of years, each squire being brought up and trained to live in the service of the estate – has assured that the family estate will continue as it has thus far continued. The Acland estates will live, in the care of the Trust. The cottages will continue to be repaired and improved, the farms will be farmed in accordance with the rules of good husbandry, the timber will be properly cared for, replanting will accompany felling; there will be security for farmer and farm worker alike, within the scope of the National Trust. (The Trust cannot control markets; not yet, anyway.) The National Trust will be able to maintain the immemorial beauty of the Acland estate, because the National Trust does not pay death duties.

No one man, however provident and spare-living, can successfully manage such estates today without a large private income. Here are a few facts about a small property in Norfolk before the war. The landlord, for his 240 acres, received a rent of £100 from the tenant-farmer. Of this, £79 had to be paid in tithe. Drainage rates took another £13. Then there was income tax at 6s. 6d. in the pound, or £32 10s. on the rent received, which was unearned income. On top of this was the Land Tax of 1s. the acre on the rateable value, which was another £3 6s. Add up these 'outgoings', and offset them against the rent received, and it will be found that out of £100 each year the sum of £127 16s. had to be paid.

Thus, by occupying the much-criticised position of Lord of the Manor, the owner was £27 16s. out of pocket every year. How about if the roof blew off the corn barn, and £200 had to be found to restore the rotten timbers and replace the shattered tiles?

In districts where the lordship of an estate had decayed through poverty brought about by death duties, a sale was inevitable. Usually a group of speculators would try and get hold of it at the auction. They did not try to get the land for its own sake, but to make money out of it by a quick resale. Perhaps there was the mansion, which no one would be foolish enough to buy to live in. That would be bought by a builder, his eye on the tons of lead on the roof, the hundreds of fine doors – oak, teak, mahogany and pitch pine – and the panelling, and, of course, the valuable moulded Italian ceilings. After these things were removed the floors would be torn up and thousands of planks, joists, purlins and rafters resold in lots. The shell of the house was left, to fall down; to be covered with brambles and ivy.

Trees in the park, planted to beautify rural England, were thrown, after being sold to the saw-mills. Hire-purchase houses in rows appeared. The farmlands, which nobody wanted ('farming in England is a mug's game'), were sold off without reserve, perhaps to the depressed-looking tenants, who bought them on a mortgage. The speculators had cleared their purchase money by the timber, the lead and the doors of the mansion, and the sale of Desirable Freehold Building Plots; the farms were, in the phrase of speculation finance, 'jam'. They departed, and sought about elsewhere for another estate coming into the market: an estate debilitated by death duties.

In southern parts of Britain many fine estates have been saved from speculative knackers by being bought by rich business men, who set about to improve them, to rebuild and recondition cottages, to restore farmhouses, and generally to try and improve their new properties.

There they would relax, and end their days, before handing on to their sons. For two or three hundred years 'merchant princes' have been doing this. Lately, such model estates were seldom self-supporting. They were subsidised out of trade or industry. I know of one gentleman who had a famous herd of cattle, which won many prizes; everything in his park, mansion, farms and estate cottages was as it should be, the admiration of all and the envy of many; but the famous herd did not pay for itself. Dividends from industry – industry depending on foreign trade, which itself depended on the import of cheap foreign food – paid for the lovely herd, as it paid for the beautiful appearance of the trees in the park. Not a bough fell but the broken stub of the limb was sawn clean, and treated with Stockholm tar.

As one man owned the entire village there was no need for those little cast-iron notices on that estate,

NO LITTER

Penalty £5

One central authority, the estate agent or steward, decreed that pits for old bottles, ashes and cans, should be dug, and the trash buried. The tenants were proud of their fine cottages, of their gardens, of their annual flower and vegetable show, of their cricket team, of their green with its pavilion and tea bar, of the new village hall where dances and whist drives took place. Most of them worked on the estate.

This was, as has been mentioned, a subsidised landed property. It pleased the efficient business man to see things neat, clean and happy-looking, so he cheerfully spent £3,000 a year from his industrial income. Even so, there were some who, peering over his park railings and seeing the tame fallow deer, considered him to be, by the very fact of ownership, one of the enemies of the working man.

February 7, 1944

The Untidiest Nation?

A correspondent writes to me from near Swaffham, saying: Can nothing be done about the chronic untidiness of the average English village? As it happened I went for a walk the day after receiving the letter. It was a Sunday, the last in January this year, and like a day of spring. No, it was better than a day of spring, for it was so unexpected, and came after days of a gale blowing from the south-west. The sky seen through the latticed window was a pale pearly azure, and every tree on the hill across the valley was distinct, as though seen for the first time by a man who had been temporarily blind. Perhaps I was that man; because for more than four weeks I had been writing all day, from about half-past nine every morning to midnight and beyond. The writing-table had been farthest from the window, out of the draughts to the open hearth, and owing to dull skies the electric light had been on both by day and by night.

But now the book was finished, and a difficult job it had been, the eighth or ninth revision of a present-time chronicle, the theme of it being that, as Waterloo was said to have been won on the playing fields of Eton, so Singapore, and all the disastrous events preceding that episode of national despond, had been lost on the fields of a Norfolk farm, or any street in the City of London for that matter. It was difficult to write because living history is almost impossible to see in true perspective, even history of a scrupulous and circumscribed sort.

The last day of January was mild and the sky was of a clarity which revealed all the details of the southerly aspect from the farmhouse window. So who was for a walk along the edge of the marshes, to the sluices, and if the smallest boy can walk so far, to Morston, and a glass of ginger beer in the inn?

Beautiful weather, no likelihood of frost now – but the new disc harrows have arrived, and will do the work of the laggard frost! Let's forget the farm today, and Time also, and take a loaf and a piece of pork (for we killed a pig last week) and some pickles in a little jar, and

139

leave without further ado, before the sun begins to decline over the hill.

The small boys carried haversacks on their backs, much easier than having them slung on the hip. Which way? Bangey Lane? Wry faces: not popular! Of course, that was where the village night-cart was tipped, on the flat ground. Why not on layers of straw, we have always wondered, thus absorbing the noisome nidorous effluvia, and also helping to make some useful compost, which the adjacent light soils, owned by the Ecclesiastical Commissioners, badly needed. All the village trash was tipped there; ashes, broken bits of glass, tins, and other inorganic rubbish. Plowing that bit of land for a neighbour, on two occasions, the rubber tyres of the tractor were cut, pierced, and punctured. At least it saved the feet of horses. The glass is scattered all over the fields, and one has to think twice before offering to help with plowing on such land.

Avoiding Bangey Lane, then, we followed the road for a bit, with the stream below, until we could cut across a field where small swedes were growing, and a lot of spurrey. Acid soil! Proceeding down the headland, we came to the Greens, where village sportsmen with rusty guns were prowling, for anyone can shoot there.

The sky was a deeper hue now: the pearly effect was gone, and a slight wind was blowing. The tide was going out; the sward on which we walked was wet and slippery. Far out to sea, across the marshes now echoing with practice gunfire, hundreds of seabirds were swirling and settling, as though among a shoal of small fish. During the last war fish increased around the coasts of Britain, when the mine-sweep took the place of the trawl net. The muddy channel we were approaching looked to be full of fish-food – worms, cockles and shrimps. Should we try one day with the rods, put away since Devon days? Visions of gleaming fish made the little boy's eyes to shine.

The river-water, penned up behind the sluice-doors at high-tide, was now pouring through the doors. The boys found corks and feathers, and amused themselves by throwing them at the iron tunnel entrance and watching them hurtle down under the current-slanted doors; while I made a plan what to do if one fell in. This happened once, in Devon, in a mill-race when one five-year-old was alone with a couple of two-year-olds. I had, as it happened, told the five-year-old what to do if ever 'one of our babies' fell in; to go downstream and pull him out at an eddy. So the five-year-old had waited below a wooden plank crossing the mill-stream, grabbed his small brother by his long golden hair, and towed him to the bank, while the baby's rubber boots were sucked off by the current into the water-wheel below. After that, the five-year-old had carried his brother home the best part of a mile, while trying to tell a soothing story to the other screaming mite clinging to his free hand.

But no mishap today. Continuing along to that ginger beer, we passed an area on the common, about half as big as a tennis court, where broken bottles, ashes, old vegetable parings, tins and cans were strewn obscenely. Farther on, along a lane leading to the hamlet, so beloved of painters, load after load of the same stuff had been tipped, under the hedge. It is said that the English are the most unmusical nation on earth; are they the untidiest? For almost every village in the country, which means the Parish Council, appears to lack the slight civic sense to have pits dug for its rubbish to be properly buried. When the first pit is dug anywhere in rural England, then the historian will know that the first step has been taken to build the New World, the planning of which is at the moment the subject of so much print and paper.

February 14, 1944

Spit and Polish

A few months back, when plowing the steep hilly slopes of old grass on the farm, I wondered what we should do when the time came to make the seed-bed for the oats and peas which I intended to sow for silage. It was difficult plowing, and many of the furrows rolled back, leaving the grass, or 'flag', on top. Other furrows lay on their sides. It took me several hours to adjust the plow to correct this, for the plow-setting was tricky, and had been altered previously by someone who did not understand that an eighth of an inch turn either way would cause an inch variation either way in the furrow slice of both plows.

The position of the plows on the beam, too, had been altered, so that many positions had to be tried before the combination was found. I did this after about forty stops; then unknown to me, my eager successor, thinking the plows were still out of alignment, tried his hand at aligning them, with the result that we were, as it were, all at sea again; the furrows twisted and heaved behind the tractor like little waves tumbling on the seashore. In this way the rest of the slopes had been plowed, and most discouraging the result looked.

However, a set of disc harrows arrived in time to start work on the untidy mess during the dry days at the end of January. What a splendid invention is the disc harrow! I wondered however I had managed to work without them for so long.

The principle of the disc harrow is that, instead of iron teeth of an ordinary harrow dragging through the soil, like a big rake, the thin steel wheels or discs, turning on an axle, do in one forward movement the work of innumerable ordinary harrowings. There are four axles, with four sets of discs. These axles can be turned inwards or outwards, thus regulating the width of the 'stroke' of the revolving harrows. Friction or drag is reduced because each disc turns round as it harrows; the power absorbed by the drag of ordinary harrows is used in the taking of a wider stroke.

With the new disc harrow the tumbled furrows were easily cut and broken up and a fine loose tilth left behind. After the heavy roll had gone over the tilth, followed by another disking, there was my seed-bed for oats and peas.

Walking round the farm, with Macinaw coat (from Canada) button'd against the shear of the cold wind, I saw that wireworm had eaten much of the wheat drilled on a field in November. Birds, too, had taken their toll. A couple of acres looked very thin. Owing to an error, the seed was drilled, not 16 pecks to the acre, as ordered, but about 10. The extra six pecks had been ordered as a present to pheasants, wireworm, rooks, jackdaws, starlings, and other gentry of the black market. Those extra pecks were still in the barn, in sacks that had been tunnelled by rats, those racketeers who are always with us. This was annoying, especially as it had occurred several times before, despite the order that no corn was to be kept in the barn in sacks.

No manure is so good as the farmer's foot; and the farmer's foot had been elsewhere, on the rail of the refectory table, with piles of manuscript before him.

During my inspection, I noticed also that the guests in khaki, who have dwelled for some years now in the corner of one field, had been tidying up the surrounding areas of their temporary abode. Gaps in the hedge had been stopped by strands of barbed wire, old glass jars and tins had been collected, rubbish from my sandpit, used for building sand, had been removed. That seemed to me to be the right spirit.

I shall always remember with gratitude a visit of the Derbyshire Yeomanry to the farm in 1941, with their armoured cars. The worst was feared, for they were numerous; but when they left, not so much as a cigarette package was left on the grass under the woods where for some weeks they had camped. The officers were punctilious, the men were helpful and friendly. They were dark days, in 1941, ending in the fall of Singapore; but these fellows gave one hope for the future. It was with added pleasure that this farmer read in the newspapers a year and a half later that the Derbyshire Yeomanry was the first British regiment to reach Tunis, upon which the entire Afrika Korps, a first-class opponent, surrendered.

Tolstoy wrote that before soldiers could be made into good soldiers they had to be brutalised. In the Prussian army in his time, all recruits were flogged as soon as they appeared in barracks. It was part of the hardening or brutalising method, to get men to stand up to fire, to do things against their natural grain, but with modern speed and *esprit de corps*, which enables generals to be recognised as true leaders of their men, the brutalising theory was seen to be obsolescent. I write as a mere civilian; but I have been with men falling under a barrage and cut down by machine-gun fire. In my youth, too, I saw drill sergeants of the Brigade of Guards with bloody finger-nails, after demonstrating to recruits how to slap the butt of the rifle at the command to Present Arms. During the Great War, the Guards Division was the one infantry division in the whole of the five Armies of the British Expeditionary Force which never failed to take its objectives. It was checked once, at Bourlon Wood in 1917, but it had been ordered to do the impossible – to make a salient out of a salient. Its flanks were in the air, which meant that shells and bullets were coming from in front and from either side of the men. It had to withdraw.

'Spit and polish' was derided until Dunkirk, even as the military virtues were discredited during the uneasy years between the wars. War is boredom, fear, anguish and misery; when the military virtues are employed in the work of truly peaceful living, then, I believe, men will be happy. Which means for myself, that my shoes must have more mud on them, and my fingers less ink.

February 21, 1944

Odds and Ends

There have been on my mind for some time now certain things I have wished to say, but have lacked time in which to do more than think about them. The first thing was, with the Editor's permission, to use this Monday's space to ask various correspondents their forgiveness for the neglect in not replying to their letters, or in acknowledging receipt of various pamphlets and books. Four poets await a verdict on their verses, two from the Eighth Army. Here is one:

> I've had a talk with Fluffy Flea,
> There's no love lost betwixt her and me;
> She dodged my blows across the bed
> And in a biting way she said:
> By reason of multiplication
> We are by far the greatest nation.

Another –

> All day, all day
> I heard the cry of waters in the brook;
> Dashed hopeful high with a wailing cry
> Of Whence? Whence?
> And perching there, where the wild crags fall
> From the heavens bare, in a shear bleak wall,
> The waters paused, looked sad around, and moved
> Disconsolate again, till spying swift
> The barracking drift, of the spray by the waters fall,
> Dived wildly on, in a body strong,
> To the soaring, wildly roaring,
> To the fever of the flood,
> That fell, still questing,
> To the new world, down the hill.

That is anthropomorphic emotion, endowing inanimate objects with human feeling, permissable to the poet. The verses have a hint of the poignancy of ordeal by battle. A third is lyrical –

145

At early morn
At palest dawn
When cirrus clouds
Hang floating high
Incandescent
In a pale blue sky
And the pale wind
Loves the sea
Then through the window
Comes a seagull's cry
Drifting loose
A bodiless sigh
A wail
Hanging thin in the air
An empty trail
Of sound.

Then there are the pamphleteers. Let's take a look at the top ones on the pile. *Runnymede Reversed*, no author named, published by the 18b Publicity Council, Woburn Square, London, WC2. I am asked to send 4d. for it, or else return it. Expertly assembled, as by a legal mind, it will be one of hundreds forming a little specialist literature for scholars of the future, when Magna Carta is restored to us again. With it is *Shall Justice Prevail?* by Ernest Dudley, on the same subject; and *Magna Carta in the Dustbin*, a companion pamphlet. Then comes *Justice for Agriculture*, by Austic-Layton, apparently a Norwich author, no publisher's address given, 2s., proceeds to the Royal Agricultural Benevolent Institution. I now have a collection of over one hundred New Britain plans, ranging from Anarchism to restoring the Stuart dynasty, from turning all small farms into one big communal farm to breaking up all big farms into 20-acre holdings to be given to the labourers. Now may I get on with my own work, please?

My eyes are dim, I cannot see
I have not brought my 'specs with me.

Also unacknowledged is a gift of the text of the Pope's broadcast on September 1st, 1943, sent by an aircraftman in the R.A.F., a brave and beautiful utterance.

One day, too, I hope to have time to read *Wild Bird Protection in Norfolk, 1943*, which comes from the Norfolk Naturalist Trust. Among the new books sent for reading, with kind inscriptions from the authors, are *Journal of a Husbandman*, by Ronald Duncan, which should sell well, and *The Snow*, by Crichton Porteous, author of *Farmer's Creed* and *Teamsman*, a writer who is also good reading because he has experienced what he writes about. Letters must go to both of them; but there is already a long queue for reply, including two from Lieut.-Col. F. Yeats-Brown, D.F.C. ('Bengal Lancer'), back in India, an old friend; another old friend, John Heygate, in Colombo with the A.A. guns, a dozen and more from pilots and soldiers in Malta, Africa and elsewhere; two Guardsmen on active service, nine prisoners of war, an amusing letter from A.J. Munnings, R.A. (weeks old; why don't you write autobiography A.J., you have a fine talent for words?) in a valley below Exmoor; several scrawly letters, beginning 'Dear dad,' from schools at North Walsham and Wantage; one from California from Mrs Robert Donat (Robert's son John acting with Charles Laughton) and, I am ashamed to admit, fifty or sixty more from kind readers of books, and also from Norfolk people making shrewd and just criticisms of various errors in the Monday articles!

Having said all that, now I want to ask some questions. One is: Were the two quails shot in the Cley-Stiffkey district last June a pair; on whose land were they shot? A further question is: With thousands of mice in the woods and fields, should not kestrels be encouraged, rather than shot? Is the rat of more danger to game birds' nests, or the kestrel?

February 28, 1944

Journal of a Husbandman

A pleasingly austere little book arrived from the borders of Devon and Cornwall to the threshold of the farmhouse the other morning. I thought to myself, Oh, another farming book, another amateur trying to reclaim derelict land. There have been many such books. For the past two months I had been writing hard myself, and wasn't in the mood to look at another man's mistakes and struggles. But when I opened the book the print at once held my attention. The author was trying to buy a small farm in North Cornwall, 'consisting of four rectangular marshes which culminated in a swamp,' from a horse dealer, called The Fox, alternatively The Grin. The author wondered if it had ever been a farm.

> An occasional gatepost reinforced my optimism. Obviously something had been kept there since the dinosaurs. And my companion said: 'I mind the time when my father kept eight cows here, and that meadow turned out a master rick of hay.'
>
> 'Then why did you let it go like this?' I asked. The Fox stopped. He grinned, not out of embarrassment. He just grinned.
>
> 'But surely,' I continued, 'even if this place couldn't pay you to run as a farm again, if you had kept it cut and the hedges steeped you would have been able to let it, or to sell it to me at a higher price?'
>
> 'How was I to know you'd come along?' he answered.

The author told The Fox that he could not, after all, buy the farm, as he had only £525. The Fox seemed surprised; and at once sold him the forty acres for £525.

The new farmer had to cut his way to the farmhouse with a billhook.

> The windows had fallen in, the doors had fallen out. Slates had slid into gutterings, gutterings swayed in the wind. Pigs had been kept in the living-room and, as though it were an advantage, the owner pointed out that a concrete trough had been made on the living-room floor. With his stick he pointed at it through a foot of dung.

148

As might be guessed, it was wanted, that farm, for an experiment in community living. The community assembled, bit by bit. One of the amusing characters arrived, in the form of Leonard Stanelly, the Communist. Here is his arrival:

He is very much a Londoner, wears hat and gloves and carries a portable typewriter. And amongst his luggage was the Communist's portable dogma: the works of Lenin, Mr and Mrs Sydney Webb, Strachey, and the poems of various fashionable sentimentalists of the proletariat. Stanelly himself has no striking features or characteristics. As far as I can gather, his parents own a large number of automatic cigarette slot machines, and Stanelly has previously been occupied in looking after these things. I am anxious to know the precise reason why he has come here. He seems equally anxious to know what I 'stand for'.

They hack their way into the fields and buy a cow. Before it dies of red-fever Leonard is told to drive it home. He arrives at the farm five hours late, having lost cow, temper and spectacles. Leonard has the job of milking the cow next day.

At nine o'clock he was still in bed. The cow should have been milked at eight. John (a pacifist) called up to him, 'Comrade Leonard, the Communist revolution has arrived.' Snores. At nine-thirty he called up again, 'Comrade Leonard, the counter-revolution has arrived.' More snores. He milked the cow, and called up – 'Comrade Leonard, the status quo has been re-established.'

Others, driven by their ideals towards a new life, arrive. Some never wash. They object to plastering walls, feeding the horse (the cart-shafts had broken soon after it was taken away from an auction) and also the cow. They sit by the driftwood fire and talk. One of them giggled.

I suppose I am regarded as a school master. Unless we can get on a better base than this, it would be better to abandon it and let owls move in again and rats rent.

The author concludes that they are a lot of intellectual nitwits. They cut bracken on the steep field. The cutter drags the horses down the hill. They also crop the land.

We are laboriously planting potatoes, one making the hole with a crowbar, the other dropping the seed in. We have no other implement.

The farmer wonders if it will pay. At any rate, he does not pay any wages. They are to share profits. At one time he says he would be content just to get his seed back, meanwhile having seen the land in cultivation. They have a mason, deaf from the last war. When the present war breaks out, Mr Tyle remarks: 'All is not what it would appear to seem.' The Tyles live in an old lorry which had been partly cemented up to comply with local building requirements. At length the removal of this Ancient Monument is threatened. Mrs Tyle wanders away with half a dozen children, leaving others behind, but returns later. Meanwhile Mr Tyle offers to build a cattle shippon, with loft, for nothing.

During harvest a spare part broke on the farm lorry. Telephone calls followed.

A spare half-shaft was eventually located at a car dump, graveyard for automobiles. A gypsy-like ferret of a man has filled a field with these hideous rusting wrecks; some lurching into ditches with their radiators off and their tyres down, others sprawling about spewing their engines out in a riotous automobile brawl. The gypsy led us through his fantastic collection to an old grandmother of an omnibus without any wheels on and a chimney stuck through the roof. He went through some papers and announced that I could either pay 7s. 6d. for a secondhand Sunbeam shaft or £2 for a whole Sunbeam of the same era as the one we already own. This was luck. And there the car was, a citadel for broody hens, complete with all fittings and an electric cigar lighter.

The whole book is penetrating, witty, and at times savagely truthful. Mr Duncan has apparently made good, for he started before the beginning of the war, and he is still on the farm; though most of the community has departed, in various states of disillusion, otherwise lack of will to work. The book is the best of its kind I have read since the classic *Chronicles of a Clay Farm* and Adrian Bell's *Corduroy*, and I now go about recommending it to my friends as a cure for their own dejection when they feel they are 'in a muddle'. It is published by Messrs. Faber, costs 8s. 6d., is called *Journal of a Husbandman*, by Ronald Duncan.

March 6, 1944

Fuel for the Cutting

In the intervals of spring cultivations we try to improve our little parcel of England. Already we have done much; but not so much as we wish. And not all the work was good work. Take the gateposts, for example. Six years ago eleven pressure-creosoted posts, hanging with eleven new gates and clapping posts, were set in place of eleven pairs of posts and gates which were fallen and decaying in the nettles. This work was done by a contractor, who charged a guinea for the labour of hanging each of the eleven gates, in addition to the cost of posts and gates. Today some of those posts are already rotten and have fallen. In future we shall use our own oak and not employ professionals.

Most of the great overgrown hedges have now been cut, laid, and trimmed. The wood of the 'bull thorns' has kept us warm in the farmhouse for three winters; and the heap is still considerable outside the circular-saw shed. We like our hedges straight; we want to plant beech in the gaps – the chalk soil welcomes the beech – and there is no hedge like a beech hedge. No fire like a beech wood fire, either.

Why not wood from one's own farm? Why coal, when fuel lies for the cutting? It depends if farming is a way of life, or a mere business, an effect of counting-houses and the industrial revolution. One of the effects of that revolution can be seen today just outside the village, on a well-known landmark where the Danes were supposed to have made a strong-point a thousand years ago – tens of thousands of tins dumped there, tins once containing food from abroad. Shades of Merrie England!

How many farmhouses burn wood today without use of coal? For myself I feel it would be immoral to bring coals from Newcastle with my hedges untrimmed, because it 'doesn't pay' to cut them. Too much has been thought of what does or does not 'pay'; and we are settling up for that thought today. Or youth is, for us.

The more coal is sold the better for trade. Burn it up, squander its by-products further to pollute the air of cities. The more housing

151

estates, cardboard, asbestos and coke-breeze, the better for trade. Cheaper barley from abroad, cheaper chilled beef from the Argentine, more and more tinned food, cheaper and cheaper cotton shifts from the East, all good for financial capitalism.

It used to be said by serious politicians that it 'paid' to give the dole rather than to scheme to give work, otherwise life, to the unemployed. Will all that come back? Some say it is already being prepared.

Meanwhile we get on with improvements while the weather delays work on the five-per-cent arable. We like our roads free of mud, our hedges trimmed and straight, our sacks folded up, our corn barn waterproof, our drains clear, our molehills chain-harrowed, our muck in shady, square heaps, our fences real fences and not trash-dumps and old-iron museums, our gates hanging (and closed). We like to think that our willow trees, planted by the river for pollards to improve the amenities of the valley, with its views from the road, will not be hacked off and destroyed again this year. They were put in way back in 1938: one thousand two hundred willow slips. Our efforts to beautify a decadent bit of England were resented by the mud-rakers, who cut them down. Two only have been allowed to grow.

Must an English trout-stream always look like a canal – sluggish, muddy, and foul in hot weather – with bubbles of decay arising, and seldom a true, ephemeral water-fly to grace the pure air of heaven? See what is poured into the noblest English river, Thames, and there's the example and answer.

Money, anything for money; nothing undertaken unless it pays! It paid to have the bones of the slain dug up from the field of Waterloo, brought to England, ground up in bone-mills for phosphate for wheat – and then squandered down the sewers into 'sweet Thames' of Spenser's poem. The scientists call us *homo sapiens* – man the wise – but some say *homo rapiens* – man the despoiler.

Will these things always be? I think not. Will salmon be leaping again one day by London Bridge? I think so. Then the pollard willows will beautify our little valley, and their roots will be growing, like Keats' daisies, from the dust of a poet's heart.

March 13, 1944

Pleasant and Unpleasant

It is sometimes said to me, 'Why don't you write more of pleasant things? You once wrote a book called *Tarka the Otter*, which took us away from the drabness of everyday life. Why don't you write another? What about the lark in the sky? Don't you ever hear it singing? Isn't the wheat still green in the fields?' My critic goes on to say he is weary of the times, and their turmoil, that he wants to be transported from drabness and unpainted streets and gaping ruins into the fair English countryside. People, he declares, are hungry for Nature (there being no more decent cocktails) and for the things of earth. Why don't I do my stuff?

I suppose the poet, the sensitive observer of wild life, was a solitary in the first place because he reacted from the ways of mass-men; because he grew up on the battlefields, disliked the mentalities which he encountered afterwards and recognised as having helped to prepare such a world for youth, and so betook himself off to the wilderness, where otters scratched up stones in streams for eels and miller's-thumbs (or loaches), where he could walk for hours without seeing a human being, listening to the lark in the sky, watching the wind-wave in the shining wheat of April, and finding solace in such things because pavements of cities were the denial and negation of their very existence.

In course of time he wrote of what he had seen, and found a kindred spirit here and there; or one who appeared, for awhile, to be the same. A few years went by, and with the popularity of the motor car townspeople began to discover the countryside. More and more acquired a habit of spending week-ends there, in refurbished labourers' cottages; and so country books, which were a bore in the 'twenties, became mildly interesting in the 'thirties.

A chance acquaintance on a heather hill above the most beautiful bay in the West of England actually uttered these words, 'Yes, I read your book, very beautiful. So this is the place I read of! Well, I flatter myself I am a beauty-lover; but if this place is going to be spoiled I may as well get in first.' He was a successful builder.

During days in the wilderness the poet sees otters, birds, flowers and trees, and teaches himself to bring the living actuality of these natural things into words on paper. When he has learned his art, the phase of solitariness ends when the poet has established himself, by his work, in the world of men. Thereafter, he moves on equal terms in the world of men; and in course of time that world, being based not on natural truth, inevitably decays. He sees the drabness, the unpainted streets, the gaping ruins, he hears the thunder of bombers and not the song of the lark, he realises that this thunder is but an effect of the ways of living which he once rejected, seeking solitude or escape from the chaotic mental world of the cities.

By his extra sensitivity, which enables him to use words to convey a living actuality, he feels the present effects of decadence perhaps more keenly than most. How then can he continue to write as though these things did not exist in his consciousness?

Art does not flourish in a war, especially in a world war. This war is so terrible that even a deliberately hashed-up musical entertainment like *Chu Chin Chow*, which outlasted the war of 1914–18, cannot be devised by those of the theatre who write deliberately for money. Hence the dearth of new plays, new music, even new songs. I have heard most of the tunes of 1914–18 over the radio of this war. The old ballads are back in the concert halls. Producers wait for plays that aren't being written. Even war-poets, who told the truth about the last affair – Wilfred Owen, Siegfried Sassoon, and prose-writers like Barbusse and Duhamel – aren't duplicated in this war. They are there, somewhere; they will be articulate afterwards; but today they are voiceless, subdued, dumb.

There is or was a literature – at any rate a spate of books – about certain aspects of the war, but they aren't even looked at any more. Most of them anyway were fakes. Their details were all the same; variations on the corpse-factory theme. They were phoney. One felt it in the personality of the writer in almost every page. They were all the same; they were not sincere. They were exploiting a market; making money out of an aspect of the war. The books I mean, added together, aren't worth one English soldier's determination to do what he is told, and hang on to it, even to his life's end.

There is a beautiful simplicity about the lives of wild birds and animals. An old soldier, who had fought with the Ghurkas and lost a leg and been much decorated, once said to me that he could never hunt an otter, or a fox, or shoot a wild bird; because he felt that they were incapable of meanness. They were essentially innocent. They lived close to life and death, and they lived intensely; they were only corrupted when they became the pets of man, exploited by man.

The world today is too far gone for the simple nature writer to function as though nothing else were happening. Only a half-wit, or a very selfish man, could behave or think without care of what was happening almost everywhere on the earth and in the air and the water. Wilfred Owen, the greatest poet of our age, whose poems were published after his death in action, left a fragment of paper among his things on which was written: 'These poems are not for this age. They may be for the next. These poems are in no sense consolatory. All the poet can do today is to warn.'

> Let the boy try along this bayonet blade,
> How cold steel is, and keen with hunger of blood,
> Blue with all malice, like a madman's flash,
> And thinly drawn with famishing for flesh.
>
> Or lend him to stroke these blind, blunt bullet heads,
> Which long to nuzzle in the hearts of lads,
> And give him cartridges of fine zinc teeth
> Sharp with the sharpness of grief and death.
>
> For his teeth seem for laughing round an apple,
> There lurk no claws within his fingers supple
> And God will grow no talons at his heels,
> Nor antlers through the thickness of his curls.

In a letter to his mother, just before he was killed, Wilfred Owen wrote: 'I am a shepherd of sheep, who do not know my voice.' The voice is still unknown.

March 20, 1994

The Task of Sisyphus

This week has been occupied with drilling corn and making seed-beds, on land that is tricky, and so things have not been straight-forward. One field has five kinds of soil on it, ranging from dog-biscuit clay to gravel brash. The clay lies on a slope of 1 in 3½ at its steepest, and the progress of the tractor is anything but straight-forward; rather does it resemble a grunting crab on wheels. Fortunately the second tractor came back promptly from its repairs at the efficient engineering firm in Norwich, and so the farmer was spared what in other years he has had to endure; making his seed-bed laboriously, and then finding, before he can drill, the weather has changed and all's to do again! In the old days that hilly field was plowed by teams of bullocks, and when seed-time came everything on a large farm was put on it; teams of harrows, two-horse rolls, one-horse rolls, more harrows, several seed-drills, all going at once. Today this isn't practicable; and it wasn't practicable to grow anything there since the last war. A farmer didn't get his costs of production back. Not only is that field steep and hard to work, but it has to be 'caught right'; it has the local reputation of being too wet or slippery in the morning, and by the afternoon of the same day too dry.

A critic has written that this pen is sometimes discourteous to local farming and its ways. Perhaps Sisyphus should be silent always. He is the figure in mythology who was given the task through eternity of rolling a great stone to the top of a steep hill; and just as it was about to come to the top it rolled down again, and Sisyphus had to try, try again; for ever; I forget why Sisyphus was punished by the gods; probably it was for having been born with a sharp mind.

Mr Hudson recently made a speech in which he said that many farmers were inefficient. Mr Hudson spoke the truth. I rate myself as one of the inefficient farmers, and this is no inverted modesty; although the W.A.C. generously ranked this little holding as an 'A' farm again this year. To build up a modern efficient farm is, as I see it, a work of a lifetime, or of a life-energy. If you go in any agricultural engineer's shops you will find, for example, machinery in for repair which with a little care would never be there. The other week I saw a fairly new tractor, having the steel spokes of one wheel being cut off by an oxy-acetylene blow-pipe. That was necessary, to remove the wheel. No grease ever having been put in the hub, the hub had seized.

Many tractors go in with smashed engines, due to no oil being in the sump. Farmer Sisyphus has to endure that; or else have no one to sit on his tractor when it is repaired. Of course, all tractor drivers are not like that; there are many fine men who care for their machines. But there are many more who don't. I know it is a boring, wearisome life, to sit on a tractor eight or nine hours a day; to have to rush on while the going's good; that it is a wrench to treat your machine always as a chauffeur treats a good car. I know, too, how for years the farming industry had lost much heart, due to what the economists call 'world conditions', not to bring it nearer home. What boy leaving school would go into farming, that Cinderella of jobs, if he could get a better, that is easier, job elsewhere? And a job that wouldn't 'stand him off' in wet weather? It was easy to blame the farmer as a hard man, for that; but it is a fact that Norfolk farmers alone owed the banks, that is were in debt by, fifteen million pounds in 1938.

In that year the barley market crashed. With wages even so low as 34s. 6d. a week, barley at 15s. a coomb did not pay, except on those highly mechanised farms which never kept a beast or a muck-cart. Cheap European barley could be bought for 8s. 6d. a coomb, after coming by rail through Europe and ship to the ports. The foreign labourers who reaped that barley got about 4s. 6d. a week wages.

Some farmers wanted this cheap imported barley. Their farms were at the ports, consisting of pig-feeding factories on the very wharves. Three or four floors of pig-houses, one above the other. Was that efficient pig-feeding, or rather pork production? Some said it was praiseworthy.

These are only examples; or symptoms. Symptoms of what? Well, of what is today. That is logic; for every effect has its cause. The stone is rolling back on Sisyphus; it is exploding and destroying him. Sisyphus is Everyman, representing the burden of everyman; of man who cannot agree to order and plan; of man who grows wheat and burns it, while children elsewhere die of starvation in the streets. The burning of the wheat in times of so-called peace is directly connected with the burning of cities in time of so-called war. These things are apparent to those with eyes to see and ears to hear.

Yes, the lark sings over the wheatfield, and the leaves break from the buds in spring; the sun shines serenely on all things. We shall muddle through somehow. Meanwhile Sisyphus rolls up his burden, and then it goes down the hill again. We are all Sisyphus: Mr Gooch and his praiseworthy efforts for the workers' union; the chairman of the Farmers' Union; Mr Hudson for the 'industry'; every cowman on his stool, day after day, week after week; every 'boss' (horrid word, tough job) trying to be patient with the man who arrives late to work, day after day, week after week, month after month, year after year, and who says, when it is mildly suggested that really his pay will have to be docked, 'Well, then, I'll leave; I can get a job anywhere'; the overworked engineer in the repair shops who cries, 'Is every labourer on every farm allergic to grease and lubricant?'; the patient publisher who says, 'When are you going to write the story of Willie the Wireworm, or Bolo the Badger?'

March 27, 1944

Wandering Spirit

The light shining through the windows and glass tiles of my studio is very bright. Outside the daffodil heads are ragged. Two sacks of sugar beet seed stand on the tiled floor, opposite me. In a patch of sunshine on the pavor floor a tortoiseshell butterfly lies, the glints gone from its wing-colours. For months I have seen it, with wings closed, hibernating up one of the purlins of the roof which supports the rafters. Now, spring has come, but it is dead. As I sat here a quick shadow flitted across the patch of sunlight on the pavor floor; a bird flew in through the open window; the butterfly, expanding there with new warmth and colour, was seized. Seeing me, the bird fluttered out of the window again; and motes of dust floated slowly through the sunshafts.

Today I am an April Fool. I am a fugitive from a brain-gang. In mythology the Fool was the wise man, the wandering spirit who represented the wild feeling which is in every one; of no more use than a blown leaf or a falling feather, but calm and wise and thoughtless as all natural things. Shakespeare's fools were an expression of the poet's abdication from midnight oil and the furrowed brow.

> Hey ho, sing hey ho
> Unto the green holly.
> Though friendship is vain
> And loving mere folly
> This life is most jolly.

Shakespeare knew it all, this thing we call life.

> Fear no more the heat of the sun,
>   Nor the furious wintry rages;
> Thou thy earthly race hast run,
>   Home are gone, and ta'en thy wages
> Golden lads and girls all must,
>   As chimney sweepers, come to dust.

160

A wood fire burns in the hearth. We made that hearth of old bricks, the chimney piece is stepped up, with 20 shelves, one staggered back behind and above the other, rising a brick-course each time. Corks, feathers, seed-packets, cartridges, bits of string, a reproduction of Botticelli's Venus stand there, with postcards from various places in the world.

Someone wrote and asked would I tell them how to burn wood apparently cut straight from the hedge. Another wrote and asked me to find lodgings for them. I can't do either, by post or print. I suspect the first question was a rhetorical one; sir or madame, you must make your own fires your own way. I can only tell you that the wood we burn in our several open hearths stands a couple of years in piles like an Indian's wigwam, to season; then the 7ft. lengths are sawn on the circular saw and brought to the woodshed in a cart, drawn by a horse, and led by either a youth of 18 or an ex-youth of 66, who 'cops it in' through a latch or door in the wall. Thences two slaves haul it to this 'studio' by way of a skep basket. The slaves are aged 8 and 10 respectively. They go through a ritual in placing the logs in my 4ft. wicker basket, then depart for more; but sometimes they seem to forget, and go looking for birds' nests, which they do not pull out but leave for the rightful owners, who have made or found their own lodgings; a good example to other species, say I.

Violets in a potted meat jar glow on the window-sill. A butterfly lies dead on the pavors. Airplanes roar overhead. The unsmokable tough-guy tobacco leaves hanging from the purlins no longer sway and whisper, the wind has dropped.

Books on the shelves. An old butter-churn, its wooden grain standing out with much scrubbing (they farmed in those days) in the corner. An osier basket of thorn-logs. Four candles in silver candle-sticks on the desk, with piles of forms, accounts, letters. A string box of iron-wood from Brazil. An aluminium case of artificial trout-flies: Red Palmer, Coachman, Coch-y-bondu, Blue Upright, Pheasant Tail. A bottle of rare turpentine. Four hoes in a row. Secateurs for pruning . . . too late again this year . . . Anyway, they are past reclaim-ing, those gnarled and bitter apple trees in the garden. Old brass ships' lanterns, one red for port, the other green for starboard. More books; piles of old magazines, *The Atlantic Monthly*, *The Salmon and Trout Magazine*, *The Estate Magazine*, *The Field*. A little Norwegian scythe. An armchair in leather, scissor-jabs in one arm long since smoothed with beeswax (John at three years old), the other arm scratched by claws (various generations of kittens). On the ledges of the brick hearth, ink bottles of red, light blue, dark blue, brown, and purple – anything for variety! Peasant-made rush brushes from the Pyrenees, years ago. A goatskin for wine, same period. Pair of skis, hickory, from Hanover, in New Hampshire, New England. Beautiful reproductions of grasses in natural colour, and a hare, by a young genius called Dürer, water-colour and etching respectively, done about four and a half centuries ago and still unsurpassed. And, oh dear me, yes, a thirty-six gallon cask or firkin of perry, still waiting to be swallowed, even as the bunches of tobacco to be smoked, by a stomach tougher than mine.

In flits the bird again; a great titmouse; inquisitive, eyeing my bean-pods hanging in bunches on the beam. Down under the tiles something rustles. It's That Mouse Again! Looking for lodgings. A banging with the Pyrenean brush on the sisal-paper between rafter and tile warns him off; but he, or she, is used to all that, and trips across the south side of the roof to its front door. A queen wasp burrs at the window – it is spring.

From the little window by the hearth there is a view across the valley to the hills, which we plowed up in the winter. Half a dozen diskings and rollings went over the furrows before the peas and oats were drilled; then the heavy rib-roll, called The Killer, went over finally and put them down. Daws and rooks no longer go there; I sniped them across the valley, with a Winchester repeater rifle, and they didn't think this sporting, and have left the slopes. One caws in the walnut tree as I write. 'You phoney farmer,' it may be saying. 'Don't you know we were after the wireworms? Call yourself a nature-lover!'

April 2, 1944

Country Life

Three books have come to me for review, the first by a professional writer, the second by a professional teacher, the third by a professional shirt-maker who taught himself to make a living out of market gardening and wrote a book about it called *Spring Onions*. Nowadays writers are farmers, farmers are writers, and professors have to mend their own shirts; a glorious mix-up, as they say. If farming is in the blood, phosphate is certainly in printer's ink nowadays. Here is Mr McGuffie:

> For the grass fields I got hold of a mixture of bone meal, sulphate of ammonia, superphosphate, and a very little potash, all made up into a mixture which I applied at the rate of six hundredweight to the acre. As well as this I found some stale farmyard manure in the buildings which we cleared out and put on King's Field.

Sometimes there is a break from the details of cropping, and we get the low-down of a Brains Trust at Coventry, when that city's Dig for Victory Week was in progress, and also an inside view of a shirt factory; and from these experiences, a Future Policy of Feeding the People, with this conclusion:

> It is clear for all to see that the more food we can produce in this country the less food we shall have to import, and therefore the more shipping space will be available for armaments and men of the fighting forces.

Mr A. G. Street, writing his *Farmer's Glory* all those years ago, has a lot to answer for. Though this is but an indirect reflexion on Mr McGuffie, whose straightforward account of his successful market gardening ventures may be acceptable to a public not yet saturated with matter-of-fact accounts of such ventures based on guaranteed prices.

Good Farming is an excellent little book, one of the best of its kind that I have seen. Here are most of the facts, all in plain basic English, about Farm Machinery, Stock, Crops, Management, Does Farming Pay?, etc., with illustrations. I hesitate over the list of implements, and their cost, for a 500-acre dairy farm. One item particularly arrested my reading. One ring roller (three sections) £17 10s. The author says this is the 1939 price, and 50 per cent to 100 per cent increase is suggested for present prices. I have just bought one for £52, which is 300 per cent increase. And how they work 420 acres of arable on one rubber-tyred tractor, and a smaller row-crop tractor, is beyond my comprehension or experience.

At 3s. this little book is bumper value, and one wonders where the publishers got the paper? There are said to be two hundred new publishing firms since the war, unhampered by paper rationing which is the privilege of the older, pre-war publishing trade. When I opened this book and saw its quality of paper and binding, and the price of 3s., I thought I must have been asleep for ten years, during which time the war had ended and publishers were no longer praying not to have a best-seller on their lists. While the going is good, this 3s. book should sell like . . . modern books about farming.

My first introduction to the writing of Sir William Beach Thomas was when I saw an infantry company commander stamping on *The Daily Mail* after reading an account of an attack he had shared in, an account which told of the larks singing through the barrage at dawn. As second-in-command of that company, I had remained at the transport lines, in reserve, and I had watched the barrage from the comparative safety of three miles back. It is true the larks were singing through the colossal flickering and earth-shaking reverberation of the guns; one heard them as the barrage slacked off, preparatory to moving forward (though soon they were 'back on the first objective'). The company commander, with a hundred and fifty casualties in the company, was in no mood a few days later to read of larks singing; nor had he heard them, where 'shell-storms spouted reddest spate.' Hence the rage with which the war correspondent's account was greeted. In those days there was a mental division between the 'civvies' and the soldiers which the bombing of cities in this war has done a little, but only a little, to close.

Sir William tells us his life story. He was bred in a Sussex rectory, spent part of his boyhood in the Fens, gained a scholarship from Shrewsbury to Oxford, where he gained a running blue, became for a while a schoolmaster before going into journalism. He became one of the chief writers of Lord Northcliffe's paper. It was in the office of

The Daily Mail that I met him in 1920, during my own brief career as a Fleet Street reporter.

As a 'star' journalist, Sir William went to Australia, to Canada, to various countries in Europe, and these journeys, with England and the English scene predominating, form the base of the autobiography. Like W. H. Hudson, our author wanders and digresses, wandering from subject to subject as thought and memory come to his mind. His book is the essence of a life, rather than the life itself. One gathers he has led a full and happy life. Writing is often a compensation for the opposite of a full and happy life. Does a child sit or walk alone, its head full of fantasies, if it can play vigorously with other children? The born writer is the lonely, odd individual, who makes his or her own world, believes in it passionately, and so creates passionate belief in it, among others of a similar nature. Emily Brontë and Richard Jefferies are such born writers; they died before they could build themselves a house or a farm with the proceeds of their books. One of the best things in *The Way of a Countryman* is the chapter describing the building of a cottage, and the specification for the builder is a joy to read. The amazing thing to me (after a slight experience of building) is that the builder appears to have carried out the instructions of the architect. 'All joinery is to be knotted and primed before leaving the joiner's shop.' 'All framing is to be put together with well-fitting mortices and tenon joints wedged up solid.' Delightful reading, for one whose new windows, put in six years ago by local artistry, are already dropping to bits.

> *The Way of a Countryman*, by Sir William Beach Thomas (Michael Joseph, 10s. 6d.).
> *Good Farming*, by V. C. Fishwick (English Universities Press, 3s.).
> *Cabbages and Committees*, by Duncan McGuffie (Faber, 7s. 6d. net).

April 10, 1944